American Women's History:
A Very Short Introduction

VERY SHORT INTRODUCTIONS are for anyone wanting a stimulating and accessible way into a new subject. They are written by experts and have been translated into more than 40 different languages.

The series began in 1995 and now covers a wide variety of topics in every discipline. The VSI library now contains more than 400 volumes—a Very Short Introduction to everything from Indian philosophy to psychology and American History—and continues to grow in every subject area.

Very Short Introductions available now:

Available soon:

For more information visit our website

www.oup.com/vsi/

Susan Ware

AMERICAN
WOMEN'S
HISTORY

A Very Short Introduction

OXFORD
UNIVERSITY PRESS

OXFORD

UNIVERSITY PRESS

Oxford University Press is a department of the
University of Oxford. It furthers the University's objective
of excellence in research, scholarship, and education
by publishing worldwide.

Oxford   New York

Auckland   Cape Town   Dar es Salaam   Hong Kong   Karachi
Kuala Lumpur   Madrid   Melbourne   Mexico City   Nairobi
New Delhi   Shanghai   Taipei   Toronto

With offices in
Argentina   Austria   Brazil   Chile   Czech Republic   France   Greece
Guatemala   Hungary   Italy   Japan   Poland   Portugal   Singapore
South Korea   Switzerland   Thailand   Turkey   Ukraine   Vietnam

Oxford is a registered trade mark of Oxford University Press
in the UK and certain other countries.

Published in the United States of America by
Oxford University Press
198 Madison Avenue, New York, NY 10016

Library of Congress Cataloging-in-Publication Data
Ware, Susan, 1950–
American women's history : a very short introduction / Susan Ware.
pages   cm
Includes bibliographical references and index.
ISBN 978-0-19-932833-8
1. Women—United States—History.
2. Women—North America—History.   I. Title.
HQ1410.W36   2015
305.40973—dc23   2014028720

3 5 7 9 8 6 4 2

Printed in Great Britain
by Ashford Colour Press Ltd., Gosport, Hants.
on acid-free paper

To Barbara Miller Solomon
and our students in Soc Sci 145

Contents

List of illustrations

Acknowledgments

Heartfelt thanks to my writing group—Carol Bundy, Kathleen Dalton, Carla Kaplan, and Carol Oja—for constructive readings of the manuscript as well as warm support and encouragement while I was writing it. Thanks also to Lola Van Wagenen, who sent an enthusiastic shout-out all the way from New Zealand. Through my work with American National Biography, I was already familiar with the consummate professionalism of Oxford University Press, an impression now enhanced by the chance to work with Nancy Toff on this project. I am proud to be part of the OUP team.

As a graduate student at Harvard in the 1970s, I had the wonderful good fortune to connect with Professor Barbara Miller Solomon, who invited me to become a teaching assistant for Social Sciences 145: Women and the American Experience. In the five years I was associated with the course, I learned the basics of women's history, from Mary Wollstonecraft to Margaret Fuller to the suffrage movement and beyond. It wasn't until I began to put together the narrative for this book that I realized how foundational that introduction had been. It is a great privilege to acknowledge this intellectual debt.

Introduction

"Always ask what did the women do while the men were doing what the textbook tells us was important," historian Gerda Lerner provocatively challenged in 1981. This book answers Lerner's charge, drawing on the explosion of scholarship in women's history to which she was a leading contributor and theorist. Few fields of American history have grown as dramatically as women's history over the past several decades. Courses in women's history taught by specialists are now standard in most colleges and universities, as are interdisciplinary women's studies programs. Historians, writers, and biographers produce a wide range of scholarship on issues of women and gender. Textbooks now include full discussions of major topics and viewpoints in women's history as an integrated part of their general narrative.

Women's history is a vibrant and ongoing project, and that vitality is on full display in this survey. In historian Linda Gordon's apt image, women's history "does not simply add women to the picture we already have of the past, like painting additional figures into the spaces of an already completed canvas. It requires repainting the earlier pictures, because some of what was previously on the canvas was inaccurate and most of it was misleading." In other words, including women in the picture—the equivalent of "add women and stir"—means rethinking and rewriting the way American history is told.

As feminist scholarship has amply demonstrated, the category of women is difficult to generalize about. The greatest challenge in providing an overview of women's history is to foreground which women are being discussed and not to simply allow the better documented experiences of white, middle-class women to stand in for the rest. Therefore, this narrative highlights the diversity of American women's experiences as continually shaped by factors such as race, class, religion, geographical location, age, and sexual orientation, among others. It also highlights the moments when differences between women, such as white slaveholding women and black female slaves, or native-born social workers and their immigrant clients, call out for contrasting perspectives. Think of this project as a giant balancing act, with multiple balls in the air at once.

As its overarching theme, this survey presents "woman as force in history." Paying homage to historian Mary Ritter Beard's pathbreaking scholarship from the 1930s and 1940s, this conceptual framework highlights the contributions, recognized and unrecognized, that women have made to the American experience. Without downplaying the historical constraints and barriers blocking women's advancement, the story emphasizes women as active agents rather than passive victims in a variety of contexts throughout U.S. history. Along with that goes a commitment to see America through women's eyes.

The goal is broad familiarity, not just with the history of American women but also with the main currents and themes of American history generally. It is neither possible nor desirable to write about women in isolation from men or separate from national events and trends. Instead women's stories link to larger themes at the same time they often challenge them. For example, traditional markers such as the American Revolution, the Civil War, and

World War II are not necessarily the most useful concepts for organizing women's history and thus have not been deployed here. With women's stories fully integrated into the broader national story, the end result will be a richer understanding of U.S. history in all its complexity.

Gender is central to this conception of history. In its simplest formulation, gender refers to the historical and cultural constructions of roles assigned to the biological differences and attributes of women and men. While sex differences are presumed to be unchanging and innate, gender differences are subject to wide variations historically and across cultures because they are socially constructed. In other words, what it means to be a woman—or a man—changes over time.

Gender is an extremely important tool for the study of history, especially women's history. Because all historical actors have a gender, practically any historical question, from diplomacy to leisure to state policy, can be subjected to a gender analysis. Furthermore, gender analysis not only highlights the ways societies interpret the differences between the sexes but also shows how these distinctions can interact with and legitimize other hierarchical relations of power, such as race and sexuality.

While gender analysis has been enormously important to the fields of women's history and women's studies, we must never lose sight of the "real" women who make American history happen. These flesh-and-blood historical actors propel the story that follows, enriching and complicating traditional historical narratives while confirming that women have been central to American history from the start. To quote Gerda Lerner again: "What we have to offer, for consciousness, is a correct analysis of what the world is like. Up to now we have had a partial analysis. Everything that explains the world has in fact explained a world that does not exist, a world in which men are at the center of the human enterprise and women are at the margin 'helping' them.

Men and women have built society and have built the world. Women have been central to it. This revolutionary insight is itself a force, a force that liberates and transforms." Knowledge is power, Lerner reminds us, and history matters, especially for women, who for so long were denied theirs: "Women's history is the primary tool for women's emancipation."

Chapter 1
In the beginning: North America's women to 1750

Pocahontas is one of the best known stock characters in the history of the founding of the United States. The young Powhatan girl who supposedly saved British explorer John Smith from execution and then later journeyed to England as the wife of John Rolfe has been reduced to a conventional (and convenient) stereotype: noble Indian princess who helps white European men and thus by extension gives Indians' blessing to all that comes after.

Walt Disney made Pocahontas into a love-struck teenager, but feminist scholars see her as a much more complex character. Think of all that happened to her in the barely twenty years she lived: she literally had her feet in two different cultures, the Powhatan world in which she was raised and the English world to which she converted. And yet even as she participated in English society, she never abandoned the Powhatan spirit world that nurtured her.

Pocahontas (a childhood nickname; her birth name was Matoaka) first encountered the newly arrived English settlers from Jamestown in 1607, when John Smith was brought to her village as a captive. She was a girl of twelve, he a middle-aged man, a shaky foundation for the fateful (and likely fanciful) story of her dramatic intervention to save his life. Several years later

Pocahontas herself was kidnapped and held hostage by English captors for almost a year. In part to cement Powhatan-English relations, she agreed to marry John Rolfe in what was arguably North America's first mixed-race marriage. In 1616 the couple and their young son made the difficult sea journey to England, where Pocahontas, now known by the English name Rebecca, was treated like a celebrity. Alas, British hospitality also meant exposure to British disease, against which she had no immunity, and she died as she prepared to sail home. Instead of returning to her ancestral birthplace, she was buried on English soil.

Pocahontas was an adventurer who straddled the two cultures whose interaction determined much of the early history of colonial North America: indigenous cultures, usually referred to as Native or Indian, and the cultures of the European invaders (Spanish, English, French, and Dutch), exported in the surge of exploration and colonization set in motion by Christopher Columbus's 1492 journey of discovery. European explorers often conceived of the North American continent as "virgin land," sparsely inhabited and still largely untouched by human settlement. In fact, North America was home to a range of vibrant and complex Native American cultures that did not simply disappear once European colonizers stepped ashore.

The contact between these two cultures involved war, upheaval, and disease, as well as interaction, negotiation, and adaptation, and gender was central to the story. Whether you were male or female affected your life just as much whether you were Native or European. The contrast between gender roles in Indian societies and European ones demonstrates the malleability of concepts of gender, as well as showing how deeply invested European settlers were in theirs.

There was no simple or linear progression in women's status over the course of the seventeenth and eighteenth centuries, either for European women or their Indian counterparts. Some things changed for the better, others declined, not necessarily at the same time or the same rate for each group. By 1750, however, a vibrant colonial culture was flourishing along the Eastern seaboard, bringing prosperity and wealth to colonists who actively participated in the thriving Atlantic commercial culture.

Many older and more traditional American history texts begin with the settlements at Jamestown in 1607 or the landing of the Pilgrims at Plymouth in 1620, which gives the impression that the story only starts when the white folks arrive. Instead we will start our story with the peoples who were already there.

"Is it a bow or a sifter?" That is how the Cherokees assigned a male or female gender to a newborn infant. Bows were used in hunting and fishing, connecting the male infant to his future life in the forest and streams. Sifters were used in making bread and processing corn, linking the female infant to her future in the world of agriculture, plants, and food production. The Iroquois conceptualized life along similarly gendered lines when they personified the forest as male and the village as female. Most human societies differentiate men's and women's roles in some form or another; the key factor is how those differences are valued and enforced. In general Indian societies saw these demarcations as complementary, not a sign of the subordination of one sex to the other. As a result, women played vital and significant roles in Native cultures—larger, perhaps, than their European counterparts.

Native women played especially large roles in the active spirit world, in part because of their close relationship to the production of food as well as their reproductive roles. Many creation stories, such as the Acoma Pueblo origin myth of Tsicht'nako (Thought Woman) and the two sisters Iatiku (Mother of the Corn Clan) and Nautsiti (Mother of the Sun Clan), drew parallels between the origins of life and the germination of plant seeds, with human life emerging from the underworld like a sprout of maize pushing up through the soil. To honor this creation myth, all Pueblo infants received an ear of corn, a symbol of the Corn Mothers, who had given life not just to humans but to plants and animals as well.

The great majority of Indian tribes were organized matrilineally—that is, inheritance passed through the mother's line. Sexual activity began at a comparatively early age and was not confined to marriage. On marriage men moved into their wives' extended family networks, which often included multiple generations living together; these women's kin groups, rather than the conjugal ties between husband and wife, served as the glue of social interaction. In Indian societies the community always took precedence over the individual.

These generalizations need to be tempered by the fact that indigenous peoples never collectively identified themselves as "Indian" or "Native American," which were terms only used by the European invaders. Instead they aligned themselves with their individual tribes or the confederations to which their tribes belonged. Further belying any sense of collective Indian identity is the striking array of cultural diversity: linguists estimate that there were four hundred spoken languages in use when Europeans began showing up on the shores. There were also significant differences among various tribes, especially by region and geography. Acoma Pueblos in the Southwest practiced intensive agriculture based on the three crops of corn, squash, and beans, whereas tribes in the Northwest, such as the Nootkas, subsisted primarily by fishing. The Iroquois in New York were distinctive for the large roles women played in the tribe's governance.

On the eve of Columbus's arrival in 1492, the traditional jumping-off point for narratives of American history, the North American continent was already populated with a diverse range of native peoples and cultures. Less than two hundred years later, 90 to 95 percent percent of that indigenous population had been wiped out, partly by warfare but mainly by the devastating array of diseases that

Europeans brought with them to North America, especially smallpox, against which Native Americans had no immunity. But even in their weakened and diminished numbers, Indians were not passive victims of the colonizing Spanish in the Southwest and Mexico or the French, English, and Dutch settlers along the Atlantic coast. Instead it was the Europeans who did most of the accommodating, having to adapt to Native rules and customs in order to survive and hopefully prosper in this new environment. Most interaction revolved around trade: products such as beaver hides and deerskins in exchange for European goods such as firearms, metal tools, gunpowder, tobacco, and alcohol. The impact of these new trading patterns, specifically the incorporation of European goods into Native daily life, was widely apparent as early as 1650.

Like Pocahontas, who first came in contact with English settlers as a child in Jamestown, women were central to these encounters. The extensive and complex trading relationships that increasingly linked Indians and European settlers were often mediated by Indian women, who acted as "cultural mediators" or "negotiators of change." Their services were needed, especially in the fur trade, because economic activity was conducted by families and communities, not individuals, and because Indian tribes and European settlers brought fundamentally different expectations to the table. For Natives, the act of exchanging goods and gifts represented a way to promote goodwill within and between communities, whereas their European counterparts tended to think of traded goods as tribute or profit. Very often it was Native women who supplied the social skills and local knowledge to bridge the cultural gap.

The significance of kinship in Native communities explains the key role women played. European explorers and traders, whether they be Spanish, French, Dutch, or English, were all strangers when they showed up in a new location, but what really drew attention was the fact that they came without women. To Native

1. **This Native American couple, depicted in a drawing from Roanoke, Virginia, by John White in the 1580s, prepare to eat a meal, most likely prepared by the woman by boiling the corn to remove the hulls.**

societies structured around matrilineal kin relationships, this gender imbalance was almost unfathomable: there literally was no place in their worldview for men without wives. So in order to build the relationships they understood to be necessary for trading alliances, the strangers had to be incorporated into kinship networks, primarily through marriage to Native women or the informal arrangements that the French called *mariage a la facon du pays* (after the custom of the country). These were not casual or promiscuous relationships but solid family units that often included children adopted from the wife's previous relationships in addition to the couple's new biracial, bicultural offspring. Such relationships were most prevalent in the French fur trade but were also common between the Spanish conquistadors and Native women in the Southwest, where intermarriage produced the mixed-raced offspring called *mestiza*. In contrast, intermarriage between English settlers in New England and Native women was rare, in large part because the sex ratio in that region was fairly equal, unlike the skewed male-female imbalance elsewhere, especially in the seventeenth century.

Artifacts and archaeology tell us quite a lot about the lives of Indian women, with one glaring exception: we do not know how they felt about the middle ground they occupied between two cultures because no surviving written documents preserve their story. Instead we have the accounts of European settlers and missionaries. Luckily these documents, when read carefully, can provide a wealth of information about Native life—and just as revealing a window on European attitudes and prejudices.

European observers seemed genuinely flummoxed by Native gender roles, which were so different from their own. For example, in European cultures hunting and fishing were sporting pursuits of the upper class, so the large roles that Native American men played as hunters were dismissed as frivolous and nonessential. And agriculture, especially working in the fields, was men's work in Europe, whereas it was women's work in Native American communities, and therefore was immediately devalued by missionaries and government officials who thought men should be in charge. This cultural miscommunication was the foundation of the demeaning European image of the Indian squaw forced to work like a drudge because her lazy husband was off besporting himself in the woods. If there was ever any question about the power of gender preconceptions, the total inability of Europeans to understand that Indian cultures were organized around different and quite effective norms is a case in point.

But Europeans did not come to North America to learn from native cultures; they came to get rich. The first waves of migrants who began arriving in Virginia in 1607 were overwhelmingly male—basically a group of young men on the make who lacked good prospects back home—and totally unprepared for dealing with such necessities as surviving the winter or foraging for food. The Indians literally were their saviors.

In the early Chesapeake settlements, white women were a tiny minority and much sought after. Most white women came as indentured servants, contracting for a set number of years of service in return for their passages over; like men, they responded to the lure of starting a new life in a new country. Once their indenture was finished, they were all but assured of marriage because of a sex ratio that hovered around six to one. Despite numerous initiatives encouraging migration to Virginia, seventeenth-century Chesapeake society failed to develop strong communities based on stable families. Only in the eighteenth century did the sex ratio come more into balance.

Settlers hoped for gold to win quick fortunes, but tobacco (introduced in 1613) turned out to be the ticket to the future for Virginia, with strongly divergent outcomes for its population based on race. Tobacco was an extremely labor intensive crop, and labor was one thing the Chesapeake lacked. Increasingly, the Virginia tobacco growers bought slaves imported from Africa to fill the void. The overall numbers of slaves were still small in the mid-seventeenth century, but by the 1680s most plantations were relying for labor on enslaved Africans. Like the white settlers, the slaves in the seventeenth century were mostly men, a fact that initially impeded the formation of slave families. And yet the low rate of runaway slaves suggests the importance of family and kin networks to enslaved African Americans from the start.

African Americans of both sexes shared the hardship of enslavement, but females bore the added responsibilities associated with child-rearing and domestic life. While there was some initial overlap in the tasks performed by slaves and indentured workers, indentured women worked in the fields infrequently, while slave women regularly did.

Historians continue to puzzle over the roots of slavery on American soil, which developed very differently from the slave system in the Caribbean, with its heavy reliance on large-scale plantations and much higher numbers (100,000 slaves in the British West Indies alone in 1675). And yet the number of enslaved Africans in North America grew inexorably: from approximately 5,000 slaves in 1675 to 13,000 by 1700, 53,000 by 1730, and 150,000 by 1750. Plantation owners affirmatively chose slave labor over free labor, allowing racist assumptions to create an enslaved class of laborers who were seen (by the white owners, that is) as more suited for such menial labor. Owning slaves also offered attractive opportunities for accruing status and power in the increasingly stratified class structure. And slaves filled a labor shortage as the number of indentured white servants declined dramatically.

The legal system quickly began to differentiate between the two classes of workers: for example, a key 1662 statute said that a slave woman's child inherited her unfree status. Among other things,

The legal foundations of slavery

This Virginia statute from 1662 shows how slave status was being codified into law. It also represents an attempt to limit interracial sex between "christians" (European settlers) and Africans.

> WHEREAS some doubts have arisen whether children got by any Englishmen upon a negro woman should be slave or free, Be it therefore enacted and declared by this present grand assembly, that all children borne in this country shalbe held bond or free only according to the condition of the mother. And that if any Christian shall commit fornication with a negro man or woman, hee or shee soe offending shall pay double the fines imposed by the former act.

this focus on maternal succession basically absolved the fathers, sometimes white, from any paternal responsibility. Slaves were scattered through the rest of the North American settlements, but never on the scale of the southern colonies.

New England patterns of settlement were quite different from those of the Chesapeake. New England settlers migrated as members of families, the sex ratio was fairly even, and a stable community life was present from the very start. These families proved remarkably fecund—women typically bore seven or eight children—causing explosive population growth that put pressure on the highly compact patterns of New England town settlement. In part because of a more hospitable climate than the disease-ridden South, seventeenth-century New England settlers also lived longer: 71.8 years for men and 70.8 for women, compared with their southern counterparts' 48 and 39 years, respectively.

Religion was also far more central to the New England experience than in the Chesapeake, for women as well as for men, with churches among the first institutions the settlers established in their new communities. Religious persecution had fueled many of the original migrations; nearly fifty thousand Puritans, dissenters from the established Church of England, left England between 1620 and 1640 for destinations such as Plymouth and Boston, including an eighteen-year-old bride named Anne Bradstreet who confessed her heart "rose" (rebelled) at finding "a new world and new manners" but quickly submitted once she was convinced it was the will of God. While Puritan women could not become ministers or preach, they supplied a key constituency as church members. Religion functioned as an important solace for women as they struggled to establish new lives for themselves and their families under very primitive conditions.

Women's household labor was central to the success of the early colonies. The household was the key economic unit and the one

Puritan marriages

Anne Bradstreet's *The Tenth Muse Lately Sprung Up in America* (1650) was the first book of poetry by a colonist to be published in England. While Puritan marriages may have been patriarchal, they also exhibited strong bonds of love and affection, as "To my Dear and Loving Husband" shows.

> If ever two were one, then surely we,
> If ever man were lov'd by wife, then thee.
> If ever wife was happy in a man,
> Compare with me, ye women, if you can.
> I prize thy love more than whole Mines of gold
> Or all the riches that the East doth hold.
> My love is such that Rivers cannot quench,
> Nor ought but love from thee give recompence.
> Thy love is such I can no way repay,
> The heavens reward thee manifold, I pray.
> Then while we live, in love let's so persever
> That when we live no more, we may live ever.

where much of women's labor occurred. While seventeenth-century houses and farms were fairly simple, the profession of housewifery was highly skilled. Women's tasks involved a range of labor inside the home and in its surrounding gardens and outbuildings, such as cooking and baking, tending the fire, making clothes and candles, and slaughtering pigs and other farm animals. And yet New England households were far from self-sufficient. Just as Indians actively embraced the opportunities offered by trade with Europeans, so did colonial families seek out and embrace opportunities to buy certain goods and services and sell others rather than make everything themselves. Our picture of idyllic self-contained New England villages should instead portray them as very much linked to the world beyond their town boundaries, even in the seventeenth century.

A constant of daily life for all the colonists was interaction with Native Americans, often punctuated by bloody and devastating outcomes on both sides. At the basis of the conflict was an insatiable hunger on the part of the Europeans, especially the British, for land, driven in part by the population explosion of continued migration and family growth. And as the number of Europeans was growing, the number of Indians continued to drop, their tribes often decimated by disease and disruption. As a survival strategy, individual Indian tribes quickly learned to play colonial politics, pitting the French against the English or vice versa, and for long stretches of time European and Indian cultures would manage something akin to peaceful coexistence, only to break out into periodic conflict and bitter warfare. Examples include Metacom's (or King Phillip's) War in the 1670s and, looking ahead to the eighteenth century, the Seven Years' War (also known as the French and Indian War) from 1756 to 1763.

Both Indian and white women were often caught in these skirmishes. In 1765 Mary Rowlandson, a minister's wife, was kidnapped from her home in Lancaster, Massachusetts, and taken hostage by the local Narragansett Indians. Rowlandson spent twelve weeks in captivity, living as part of the community while constantly on the move. In her narrative of captivity, published in 1682 and one of the most widely read prose texts of its time, she styles herself as a "godly captive" who endured her trials as a test of her religious faith. When she was finally released after her husband paid a hefty ransom, she wanted nothing more to do with her Indian captors, whom she considered "murtherous wretches" and "ravenous beasts." Other kidnapped white women had a different reaction: they decided to stay with their Indian captors. For example, Mary Jemison made this choice after being abducted by the Shawnee from her home in Adams County, Pennsylvania, and then being given to the Seneca, with whom she remained. Few English men ever willingly crossed over to Indian life, being more likely to resist than adapt. Perhaps English women captives had more reasons than English men to find life better on the other side.

Despite regional differences between New England, the Chesapeake, and the Middle Colonies of Pennsylvania, New York, and New Jersey with their large representation of Dutch and Quaker settlers, the lives of white colonial women bore many broad similarities. Almost every woman could expect to be married at some point in her life, often more than once if she was widowed. Once married, her life would include productive and reproductive labor: household management and food production alongside childbirth and child-rearing. The word "spinster" comes from spinning, but there were few unattached females in the colonies because the marriage rate for native-born women was so high.

By law and custom, married women's lives in European coastal settlements followed a patriarchal model, with the husband as the head of the family and his wife and children his subordinates. That was also the model for the state, with the monarch playing the role of patriarch over his subordinate subjects. Indeed under the British common law doctrine of *feme couvert* (a married woman who was covered or protected by her husband), women lost the ability to act independently at law when they married, the assumption being (as English jurist William Blackstone famously put it) that "by marriage, the husband and wife are one person in law." And yet there were certain familial situations in which wives willingly took on roles usually assigned to men. Women married to sea captains or fur traders, who were often away for months at a time, or women whose husbands were conscripted to fight in the various Indian wars, in effect functioned as "deputy husbands." As always, there was a gap between what prescriptive literature said women *ought* to be doing and the actual realities of their daily lives, which were often more fluid and complex.

Certain disorderly women pushed the boundaries even farther by failing to conform to the values of wifely submission, general subordination to men, and religious modesty. "You have stept out of your place, you have rather bine a Husband than a Wife and a preacher than a Hearer; and a Magistrate than a Subject."

That was the judgment of Reverend Hugh Peters on Anne Hutchinson, an elite woman in Massachusetts who challenged the religious authority of Puritan elders in the 1630s by holding meetings in her home where she discussed matters of theology and salvation with her followers. Hauled before the authorities, she was run out of town for her transgressions and relocated to Long Island, where she was killed in an Indian attack in 1643.

Mistress Margaret Brent of Maryland was more an extraordinary woman than a disorderly one, but she also rattled the status quo. An unmarried woman of substantial property and standing, Brent defied gender expectations when she was appointed the lord proprietor's attorney. Based on her appointment, she petitioned the colonial government in 1647 for the right to vote in Maryland's general assembly. Her request was turned down, but the fact of her application shows how in the 1640s, class status could trump gender, at least enough to frame this unusual request.

The most disorderly and disturbing women of this period were those accused of being witches. The best known witch hunt is of course the one that occurred in Salem in 1692, but that was just the culmination of a long history of outbreaks, often at times when civil society was facing a crisis, such as deteriorating relationships with local Indians or conflicts over land distribution. Witches were predominantly women, and they were also predominantly older women, often those on the fringes of their communities for various reasons: a scold, a meddler, a troublemaker, an angry neighbor. In other words, they posed a potential threat once they made their supposed pact with the devil but were also more vulnerable to accusation because of their outlier status. And in a generational twist, their accusers were often young girls, perhaps enjoying the thrill of being the center of attention—"Whats that?" demanded seventeen-year-old Mercy Short, "Must the Younger Women, do yee say, hearken to the Elder?"—as the accusations were hurled. At Salem, 115 local residents were accused of being witches, three-quarters of them women, and nineteen were executed. Only when religious and political leaders stepped in to quell the hysteria did it end. While there were a tiny number of witchcraft accusations after 1692, Salem basically represented the end of the line. It was almost as if the colonists decided to put aside the premodern beliefs in the supernatural that were common to rural agrarian communities in favor of a more secular approach to civic life.

Salem witchcraft

In 1692 Cotton Mather described Mercy Short's possession by witchcraft in "A Brand Pluck'd out of the Burning," which included a verbatim transcription of a "fit" she experienced while bewitched. Several years before Short had been taken captive by Indians. She escaped, but her parents and several of her siblings were murdered.

Oh You horrid Wretch! You make my very Heart cold within mee. It is an Hell to mee, to hear You speak so! What? Are You *God?* No, bee gone, You Divel! Don't pester mee any more with such horrid Blasphemies!...

Fine promises! You'l bestow an Husband upon mee, if I'l bee your Servant. An Husband! What? A Divel! I shall then bee finely fitted with an Husband: No I hope the Blessed Lord Jesus Christ will marry my Soul to Himself yet before Hee has done with mee, as poor a Wretch as I am!...

Whats that? Must the Younger Women, do yee say, hearken to the Elder?—They must bee another Sort of Elder Women than You then! They must not bee Elder Witches, I am sure. Pray, do you for once Hearken to mee.—What a dreadful Sight are You! An Old Woman, an Old Servant of the Divel! You, that should instruct such poor, young Foolish Creatures as I am, to serve the Lord Jesus Christ, come and urge mee to serve the Divel! This an horrible Thing!

Another manifestation of changing mores was the onset of the "consumer revolution" beginning around 1700. Historians use this phrase to convey the new focus on buying and owning things for personal and domestic use—stuff, as it were—that accompanied rising prosperity and a move beyond subsistence and survival to a more vibrant mercantile economy as well as a society more stratified by class. Here is a simple illustration. In the seventeenth century, colonial houses were sparsely furnished. Life revolved around the hearth. Families ate dinner off of a table-board topped with several trenchers containing hollowed bowls to hold the food, which was eaten with spoons; beverages were drunk from a single flagon passed around the table. Colonists, especially children, often ate standing up because there were few chairs or stools. Cooking implements were utilitarian, as was clothing. Privacy was nonexistent. When guests came to stay, they often shared the family bed.

In the eighteenth century households looked quite different, even at the lower end of the social strata. There were china plates and silver or pewter utensils for eating and chests of drawers for storing extra clothing and linens. Instead of guests being welcomed into the kitchen, they were now entertained in a formal parlor whose only function was for receiving visitors. Larger and more elaborate houses needed things to fill them up. So where did these material goods come from? The thriving Atlantic trade, which linked the American colonies to the markets of Europe and beyond. Instead of thinking of the colonies as isolated backwaters, think of them as active participants in a vibrant Atlantic culture that reigned on both sides of the ocean.

One of the most spectacular examples of this interconnected Atlantic world was the widespread dispersal and consumption of printed material. By the 1700s, colonists in Philadelphia, New York, and Boston were reading the same books and broadsides as their counterparts in London, Edinburgh, and Bath. They had

2. This fireplace at the Burrough-Steelman House in Pennsauken, New Jersey, shows the tools and utensils available to a mid-eighteenth-century housewife.

access to newspapers with information and gossip from this wider world. They could follow new fashions and traffic in new ideas.

Some of the most enthusiastic consumers of this new Atlantic culture were white women, especially those who lived in the colonies' thriving merchant centers. Women bought the china and then used it to serve tea (the quintessential consumer product, which quickly went from luxury to necessity) to their guests in their elaborately decorated parlors while wearing the newest fashions from London or Paris. While sipping their tea, they discussed the news from abroad or books they had recently read, such as Samuel Richardson's epistolary novels *Pamela: Or, Virtue Rewarded* (1740) and *Clarissa: Or the History of a Young Lady* (1748). Things had come a long way from the harsh and primitive conditions that had greeted white settlers when they first arrived in the early 1600s. The American colonies were definitely coming of age by 1750.

Midcentury is also an important mark for changing attitudes about white women's roles in colonial society. In the seventeenth century women's lives were defined by their roles as wives, daughters, and widows within a patriarchal family and state. "Women's sphere" did not exist, because women were not necessarily thought of as a separate category or entity from men. To be sure, women's lives were profoundly shaped by their gender (Native American women's lives too), but they were primarily seen as members of communities or families rather than a group apart.

By 1750, especially in the transatlantic literature that colonists were reading, it is possible to see the inklings of a new view of women: "'Tis woman's sphere to mind / Their Children and their House," wrote an eighteenth-century poet. Instead of hearty colonial housewives slaughtering livestock or fending off Indian attacks, white women were now referred to as "the fair sex," increasingly associated with the family, and less involved, at least in theory, with the broader public world. This growing split between the public and the private assigned a higher priority to motherhood as a specific role for women, with women now given large responsibilities for the moral and intellectual growth of their children, a role that previously had devolved to patriarchal fathers. A loving conjugal relation between husband and wife also became more important, with the choice of a mate now one of the most significant decisions a woman could make. And in terms of religion, women increasingly filled the pews of eighteenth-century churches and would continue to do so in the nineteenth. As congregations became predominantly female, piety became even more associated with women.

It is easier to document these emerging trends than to explain why they happened, but the changes were obviously linked to broader historical developments. The explosive growth of commercial capitalism and a thriving mercantile economy spanning the globe spread goods and ideas far and wide. The Glorious Revolution in England in 1688 transformed the relationship between monarchs and their subjects, as did the rise of Enlightenment thought, such as John Locke's *Two Treatises on Government* (1690), which proposed that political authority came from "social compacts," not divine right. Finally, a new understanding of biology and physiology after 1700 encouraged the division of humans into a two-sex model, rather than women being seen simply as lesser or inadequate versions of men. This new emphasis on difference grounded in fixed biological categories encouraged the view that women as a group were fundamentally different from—and potentially inferior to—men.

This new focus on women's sphere can be seen as diminishing women's extensive colonial roles, narrowing their lives to primarily home and family. This mindset also clearly applied more to privileged white women than to female slaves or Native American women. And yet by introducing a new concept of womanhood, the ideology fostered a sense of sisterhood that encouraged women to think of themselves as a shared group. Indeed that very gender solidarity eventually became the rationale for the birth of an aggressive nineteenth-century women's rights movement, which challenged and eventually overturned the very notion of limiting women to a restricted sphere. The emerging ideology thus opened the door for future generations of American women to take a larger role in affairs far beyond the domestic realm. This ongoing expansion of opportunities, and which women were able to seize them, and when, characterizes American women's history from the eighteenth century all the way to the present.

Chapter 2
Freedom's ferment, 1750–1848

In 1787 a fourteen-year-old African American slave named Sally Hemings journeyed to Paris as a servant in the household of her master, Thomas Jefferson, then serving as the ambassador to France from the newly established United States of America. When she returned to Virginia in 1789, she was pregnant. That child did not survive, but four other children did. Confirming generations of rumors, DNA evidence strongly suggests that Thomas Jefferson was the father of Sally Hemings's children.

Despite being born into slavery, Sally Hemings's mixed-race identity tied her intricately to the white world. Her mother, Betty, a slave on the Virginia plantation of John Wayles, had a sexual relationship with her master that produced several children, including Sally. When Wayles died in 1773, Betty and her children became the property of Thomas Jefferson, who had married Wayles's daughter, Martha, the year before. Martha Jefferson, worn out after bearing six children in less than ten years, died at the young age of thirty-four in 1782. Thomas Jefferson never remarried, an unusual choice for a man of his age and standing. One possible reason was his long-standing relationship with Sally Hemings, who was actually Jefferson's deceased wife's half-sister. The ties of slavery and bondage were intricate and complicated indeed.

Sally Hemings never spoke publicly or engaged in political acts, but she still was a significant historical figure for the role she played in the life of Thomas Jefferson, the country's third president. Her relationship with Jefferson was something of an open secret, especially with the existence of extremely light-skinned children bearing an uncanny resemblance to the Monticello master. Gossip about their relationship even played a role in the 1800 presidential campaign, yet it took almost two hundred years for the truth to be confirmed.

As a human being and a slave, Sally Hemings stands at the uneasy juxtaposition of liberty and slavery that was the legacy of the American Revolution. Her owner and the father of her children helped to conceive the new democratic experiment that became the United States of America at the same time he acquiesced in (indeed, profited from) the institution of slavery. As a woman and a slave, Sally Hemings's life story mocks the Declaration of Independence's notion that all men were created equal. Combining race and sex (two strikes against her), her life allows us to ask what slavery meant for women, white and black. Further, what would it take to win the freedom of both slaves and women, and who would plead their cause?

Just as democracy and slavery functioned as co-dependents in the early republic, so too did slavery and the early industrial revolution. Slavery produced the cotton that was sent north to be woven into textiles by the young farm girls who flocked to the new mills in Lowell, Massachusetts; the northern economy was just as dependent on raw materials from the South as the South was on northern capital and credit. So let us not draw the contrasts between a free North and a slave South too starkly. Further complicating the story is the multicultural West, whose heterogeneous populations (Anglo, Mexican, Spanish, Native American, and Chinese) were far more diverse than their northern and southern counterparts, and where gender often played out in unexpected ways.

Another defining characteristic of the early republic, especially in the Northeast, was the remarkable range of benevolent, religious, and political associations founded to confront the ills of society. White women played a key role in this reform impulse, despite the prevailing ideology that relegated them to the private sphere of their homes and families. Stretching from religious benevolence to temperance to antislavery activism and even women's rights, women's participation in a broad range of activities reminds us that the line between public and private was quite porous indeed.

Revolutionary legacies

What did the American Revolution mean to the new nation's women? In part it depends on which women. Certainly enslaved women saw little change in their status, despite the lofty rhetoric about liberty and equality contained in the Declaration of Independence. More broadly, the American Revolution did not radically change the lives of most American women, especially when it came to political rights and legal status. And yet it provided openings, especially for elite white women, to play larger roles in the new democracy. In 1798 playwright and poet Judith Sargent Murray predicted the dawn of "a new era of female history," and these changes in consciousness would play themselves out for decades to come.

Despite a prevailing ideology that defined women in terms of their homes and families, women could not have remained aloof from events leading up to the break with Great Britain even if they had wanted to. Embedded in a civil war that raged all around them and forced everyone to take sides, women tentatively began to forge a new relationship to the public realm. In Mercy Otis Warren's spirited words, "as every domestic enjoyment depends on the decision of the mighty contest, who can be an unconcerned and silent spectator?" Because of housewives' central roles as consumers, the calls to boycott imported British goods like tea and cloth would have failed without women's support. Think of

A SOCIETY of PATRIOTIC LADIES.

3. This 1775 British cartoon makes fun of the revolutionary sentiments of the "patriotic ladies" of Edenton, North Carolina. Nobody seems to notice the dog lifting his leg in the lower right corner.

these boycotts as the politicization of the household, where a simple decision about whether to drink British tea or buy a British book took on major political dimensions. Similarly, when women decided to make their own homespun cloth, their collaborative spinning bees represented a pointed anti-British stance.

The Revolutionary War temporarily disrupted gender expectations in a number of ways. Once the war officially began in 1776, patriotic women took on new roles. The Ladies Association of Philadelphia was so successful in raising funds for the army that it earned a commendation from General George Washington himself for its "female patriotism." Women whose husbands went off to war or served in the new government had to cope on their own; Abigail Adams's famous entreaty to her husband John to "Remember the Ladies" was written during one of his lengthy absences. Women married to Loyalist men who sided with the British saw their lives totally upended, especially if they did not agree with their husband's decision; their efforts to use legal recourse after the war to regain confiscated property highlighted the limits of women's independent legal standing. Finally, some women (Deborah Sampson, for example, who donned men's clothing and later received a pension for her service) actually fought in the war. More typical were the camp followers, wives and other women who trailed along with the ragtag colonial army and helped with the cooking, laundry, and other traditional female chores.

Probably the largest changes for women during the Revolutionary era were changes in consciousness epitomized by the concept of "republican motherhood." In a new democratic country, the mothers of the republic were tasked with instilling in their sons the qualities of virtue, piety, and patriotism necessary to the young country's future. And in order to do this properly, they themselves needed more access to newspapers and knowledge of current events and books. While such a role was a long way from full participation in political life, it was an opening wedge.

Abigail Adams's revolutionary call

While her husband, John, served as a delegate to the Continental Congress in Philadelphia, Abigail Adams ran the farm and managed the family household in Braintree, Massachusetts. She was also an inveterate and witty correspondent who more than held her own with her husband, who would serve as the nation's second president.

Braintree March 31 1776

I long to hear that you have declared an independency—and by the way in the new Code of Laws which I suppose it will be necessary for you to make I desire you would Remember the Ladies, and be more generous and favourable to them than your ancestors. Do not put such unlimited power into the hands of the Husbands. Remember all Men would be tyrants if they could. If perticuliar care and attention is not paid to the Laidies we are determined to foment a Rebelion, and will not hold ourselves bound by any Laws in which we have no voice, or Representation.

As a corollary, the emphasis on republican motherhood encouraged a pragmatic new interest in education for women. Granted, expanding access to education was mainly to make women better wives and mothers, but linking erudition to republican ideals made it less threatening. (Previously too much learning had been thought to unsex women, making them unfit for marriage and domestic duties.) In the early years of the republic, the topic of women's education received wide discussion, starting with the publication of Dr. Benjamin Rush's pamphlet "Thoughts on Female Education" in 1787. Soon a range of finishing schools and female academies sprang up; Emma Willard's founding of her eponymous school in Troy, New York, in 1819 exemplifies this trend. Other female seminaries followed, although confined mainly to the Northeast. As a byproduct, women found new opportunities as teachers in the expanding public and private school systems; by midcentury, a quarter of the nation's teachers were women, although the figure was much higher (four-fifths) in Massachusetts, a harbinger of the future. With a few notable exceptions, however, such as the founding of coeducational Oberlin College in 1833, the broad expansion of collegiate education for women would have to wait until after the Civil War.

While the American Revolution did not dramatically reshape women's lives, it did set in motion a range of other changes that affected the early history of the country and its female inhabitants. One of the most significant was the resumption of an expansive westward thrust after the cessation of hostilities. The original colonies, now organized as a federation of states, filled up the backcountry, burst over the Appalachian mountains, and then just kept going; a similar surge happened after the Civil War. Some of the biggest losers were the Native American tribes that had populated the land along the eastern seaboard as well as the Northwest Territory, bounded by the Ohio River. No longer essential partners for trade and survival, Native nations were increasingly seen as major impediments to land acquisition and permanent Euro-American settlement. No one asked why the space could not just continue to be shared.

The Cherokee are a case in point. The traditional Cherokee way of life had already undergone significant changes after contact with European settlers in the seventeenth and eighteenth centuries, specifically a larger emphasis on war and trade (in deerskins), which elevated men's roles relative to women, who continued their traditional focus on farming and food production, especially corn. The aftermath of the American Revolution led to new pressures on their land, which was desired by white settlers in the new state of Georgia who self-servingly reasoned that since the Cherokee were not actively cultivating all their commonly held land, they did not have a right to it. At the same time, a focus on "civilizing" the Cherokee tried to remake them along European lines, which consisted of turning men into farmers (even though this had always been women's work in Cherokee culture) and encouraging women's subservience in domestic matters. The Cherokee adapted the new ways selectively, but no matter what they did, they were in the end defenseless against an aggressive U.S. policy that mandated forced cession of tribal lands to white settlers and the relocation of the Cherokee to territory far beyond the boundaries of the United States at the time. Thus began the Trail of Tears, the forced removal of the Cherokee nation to Indian territory in the future state of Oklahoma in 1838–1839. Not only did they lose all their land, but disease and hardship also significantly decimated their population along the way.

This seemingly insatiable hunger for land had similarly deleterious effects on whichever tribes were in the way of white settlement, whether they be the Choctaw in Mississippi, the Iroquois in upstate New York, or the Sauk in Wisconsin. The new federal policy, which eventually was codified in the Dawes Act of 1887, increasingly consigned Native Americans to federal reservations, especially in Oklahoma, but also much farther west in what became Arizona, New Mexico, and South Dakota, while opening large swaths of former Indian land to white settlement. And yet despite these geographical and cultural dislocations, Native tribes still demonstrated the cultural persistence that had characterized all encounters since the first contact with European settlers.

Similar patterns of contact, assimilation, and change were at work throughout the West. Actually "the West" is a bit of a misnomer: from the perspective of Mexico, which controlled much of this land until 1846, this same territory was its northern frontier. Ever since initial contact, the dominant pattern in the borderlands with Mexico had been cultural interaction and accommodation interspersed with periods of violence and warfare. For example, during the Spanish and (after 1821 independence) Mexican occupations of what became New Mexico in 1848, an extensive system of captive exchange involved both Indian women and to a lesser degree Spanish and Mexican women, who literally crossed between cultures through capture, ransom, or sale. Then through adoption and marriage, many of these female captives stayed in their new culture, establishing families and being integrated into the community. More broadly, intermarriage between Mexican women and explorers, traders, and Natives occurred long before Anglos appeared on the scene—and continued afterward. In this fluid setting, women played critical roles as the cultural mediators between Mexican, Native, and Anglo cultures.

While Anglo traders and trappers had been exploring and exploiting western lands for decades, the white presence took a significant leap forward in 1843 with the mapping of the Overland Trail. Over the next twenty years, more than 350,000 individuals made the arduous, two-thousand-mile trip from the Missouri River across the plains and the Rockies, with Oregon and California as their goal. Many of these migrants traveled in family groups, drawn by the prospect of new lives and fertile, bountiful land that was presented as waiting to be settled. Except, of course, that it was far from empty.

A mythic view of the frontier still holds a powerful sway on the popular imagination (especially where Hollywood is concerned), and gender is central to this story. In the traditional telling, heroic cowboys, Indians, miners, bandits, soldiers, and farmers battle nature and each other as they work to "tame" the West. The limitations of this view of the American West should be readily apparent. It focuses attention mainly on the relatively short period of Euro-American western expansion and ignores the ways the American West had long been a vibrant cultural crossroads. And it represents the archetypical westerner as male. When women are mentioned at all, they fall into predictable stereotypes: the prostitute (with or without a heart of gold) and "the gentle tamer" bringing East Coast civilization to the wild and savage West solely by her presence.

Not surprisingly, the story of the women's West is more complex and far more interesting than those stereotypes, starting with women on the Overland Trail. These hardy pioneers with their sunbonnets and sturdy boots made painful choices about what to take and what to leave behind as they loaded up a lifetime's worth of possessions onto Conestoga wagons. Gender was definitely a factor here: usually it was men's decision, not women's, to seek a new life in the American West. "O let us not go," Mary A. Jones confided abjectly to her diary after her husband read a book about California and proposed relocating the family halfway across the continent. In many ways, women on the move had more to lose—their established homes, their female friends, their churches and associations—to say nothing of facing specifically female hardships on the trail, such as pregnancy and childbirth. No doubt some unwilling pioneers rued their fates every step of the way. And yet other women, either single or in families, seized the opportunities for a new life less encumbered by traditions and constraints. Women schoolteachers were an especially hearty—and valued—bunch.

Whereas families traveled the Overland Trail, it was primarily single men who joined in the Gold Rush that took off in California in 1849, causing a huge gender imbalance: women made up only 8 percent of California's population in 1850, the year it became a state. In the boomtown, get-rich-quick atmosphere, it literally was a world upside down: without women to perform traditional services like cooking and cleaning, men had to learn to do it themselves or do without.

In addition to the temporary destabilizing of gender roles, California offered extraordinary demographic diversity. Its culture was influenced by its early Spanish roots and later by dominion by Mexico. The vast majority of native Californians were of *mestizo* or Mexican background, but Anglo arrivals deployed the term "Spanish" to differentiate elite women belonging to landowning families who had married Europeans

Families on the Overland Trail

Lucy Henderson made the arduous overland journey to Oregon with her family when she was fifteen and later wrote this account of the challenges women faced on the trail:

> Mother had brought some medicine along.... My little sister, Salita Jane wanted to tast it, but I told her she couldn't have it. She didn't say anything but as soon as we had gone she got the bottle and drank it all.... When Mother called her for supper she didn't come. Mother saw she was asleep, so didn't disturb her. When Mother tried to awake her later she couldn't arouse her. Lettie had drunk the whole bottle of laudanum. It was too late to save her life....

> Three days after my little sister Lettie drank the laudanum and died we stopped for a few hours, and my sister Olivia was born. We were so late that the men of the party decided we could not tarry a day, so we had to press on. The going was terribly rough. We were the first party to take the southern cut-off and there was no road. The men walked beside the wagons and tried to ease the wheels down into the rough places, but in spite of this it was a very rough ride for my mother and her new born babe.

> After a great hardship...we finally made our way through...to Oregon it was late in the year and the winter rains had started. We had been eight months on the road instead of five, we were out of food, and our cattle were nearly worn out.... We lived on boiled wheat and boiled peas that winter.

or Euro-Americans (the supposedly "good" women) from nonelite Mexican women, whom Anglos presumed to be immoral as well as racially impure. And yet even with the creation of this faux Spanish heritage, the racial and ethnic lines in California were never neatly drawn. California at midcentury also contained as many as twenty-five thousand Chinese immigrants, almost exclusively men, who came as part of the Gold Rush, as well as a robust indigenous Native American population. Confirming a pattern that had occurred in the East and the Midwest, the relentless pressure of Anglo expansion and settlement along what was considered a "frontier" had deleterious effects on Native populations, such as the Miwok, for whom the same land was their long-established home. Anglo women as well as Anglo men reaped the rewards of the removal of Mexican and Indian populations from their ancestral lands.

In contrast to the multicultural West, race was more of a binary, black-white issue in the South. And women were on both sides of that racial divide. White southern women, whether they were members of a slave owning family or not (about one-quarter of the region's free population owned slaves), lived in an extremely patriarchal society that provided few outlets for participation in events and institutions beyond their homes and farming communities. Educational and cultural opportunities were limited, except in towns and cities, and churches did not play the central role they did in northern society. As the nineteenth century progressed, southern society turned more defensive about the institution of slavery, making southerners less willing to entertain challenges to traditional gender definitions either.

White southern women of the slave owning class lived side by side with their black slaves, male and female, their lives intertwined but uncomprehending. If a universal sisterhood united all women, one would expect to see solidarity between white mistresses and their female slaves. While scattered sentiments suggest that white women were less invested in the slave system than their men ("Southern women are, I believe, all abolitionists at heart" said slave owning Gertrude Ella Thomas of Georgia), most often these sentiments, penned privately, were directed more at the disagreeable aspects of managing slaves rather than slavery itself. White women had far, far more in common with their menfolk on the basis of shared racial and class privilege than they did with enslaved women.

Slave women's status—or more accurately, their economic worth—was inextricably linked to their ability to reproduce the slave population. That fact of life did not keep them from trying to build stable families within the institution of slavery. Most slaves were married (informally, that is, since these unions were not recognized by the law), but often to slaves on nearby plantations. (This was called an abroad marriage.) With the official end of the slave trade in 1808, the main way to meet the labor needs of the expanding southern cotton economy was through an internal slave trade; since males were more desirable as workers, they were sold to distant plantations in the Deep South at a higher rate, thereby breaking up the bonds that formed in the slave quarters. As a result the structure of many slave families was a loose extended family held together by the mother.

The daily life of female slaves was harsh. Only a few (no more than 5 percent, mainly on the largest plantations, and often the more light-skinned) worked as house servants; most toiled in the fields along with men, albeit usually in all-female work gangs. In addition to this demanding physical labor, which continued even during pregnancy and lactation, slave women were vulnerable to exploitation, sexual and otherwise, at the hands of white masters and foremen. Black women enjoyed far less control over their bodies than did white women. Sexual coercion of female slaves by white slave owners was common, producing a range of mixed-race children who kept their mother's slave status at the same time they bore the patrilineage of the master. Yet their existence, as the case of Sally Hemings and Thomas Jefferson shows, was acknowledged only obliquely. Southern slave owner Mary Boykin Chesnut captured the way white mistresses simultaneously knew what was going on while they looked the other way: "Any lady is able to tell who is the father of all the mulatto children in everybody's household but their own. Those she seems to think drop from the clouds."

Let us return to Sally Hemings to put a human face on the story of slavery, using the Hemings family as a window on Virginia plantation life and how circumstances were often beyond the control of even the most trusted (and intimate) slaves. Despite the meticulous accounts Thomas Jefferson kept of the workings of his plantation at Monticello, he was unable to keep his expenses in line with his income, so the estate began to rack up enormous debt. At one point he had to sell his cherished books to the Library of Congress to make ends meet. When Jefferson died in 1826, Monticello was in a state of fiscal and physical disrepair. His will made no specific mention of Sally Hemings; such an inclusion would have been much too public an acknowledgment of what everyone suspected. But all four of her children slipped into freedom before and after Jefferson's death, taking advantage of their light skins to simply blend into the Virginia population. Sally herself moved to Charlottesville with her two sons, where she lived until her death in 1835. Other slaves at Monticello did not fare so well: six months later at auction ("130 VALUABLE NEGROES" read the broadside), families were split up and slaves scattered to near and distant plantations, their fates largely lost to history. Even with Thomas Jefferson as a master, there was no such thing as enlightenment when it came to the institution of slavery.

The female world of work and benevolence

"Thine in the bonds of womanhood." Thus did Sarah Grimké sign a letter to a friend in the year 1838. This sense of sisterhood had its roots in the eighteenth century but came to fruition in the Northeast in the first half of the nineteenth in the concept of separate spheres, that is, the way in which women's lives were supposed to revolve around the familial and private, whereas men were expected to inhabit the wider world of politics, work, and public life. As the dual meanings of Grimké's phrase suggested, the doctrine of separate spheres both recognized the oppression of women while simultaneously suggesting a path toward female autonomy and empowerment through shared consciousness. But as an actual description of nineteenth-century women's lives, the concept remains flawed, even for the white middle-class women who were its main constituency. Instead of occupying a separate sphere based on sex, many elite women were closely linked to comparable men by race and class. And many women—slaves and free women of color, working-class women, and western pioneers, among others—were left outside this ideal entirely.

A "cult of true womanhood" defined by an emphasis on piety, purity, submission, and domesticity saturated early nineteenth-century prescriptive literature, specifically the women's magazines, books, and religious tracts dedicated to telling women how they ought to act. No one pushed this message more vigorously than Sarah Josepha Hale, the original editor of the *Ladies Magazine* (founded in 1828), who went on to spend forty years (1837–1877) as editor of *Godey's Lady's Book*. Filled with fiction, fashion, poetry, and (in the case of *Godey's*) individually hand-tinted illustrations, these periodicals both engaged and instructed the white middle-class women who were their target audiences. So, too, did some of the early housekeeping manuals, such as Lydia Maria Child's *The Frugal Housewife* (1829) and Catharine Beecher's widely read *Treatise on Domestic Economy* (1841). If women wanted to escape from the demands of domesticity, they could turn to best-selling novels, many written by women, such as Catharine Sedgwick's *New-England Tale* (1827), Sarah Josepha Hale's *Northwood* (1827), Caroline Gilman's *Love's Progress; or Ruth Raymond* (1840), or Susan Warner's *The Wide, Wide World* (1850). In a class by itself was Harriet Beecher Stowe's *Uncle Tom's Cabin* (1852), which not only was a runaway best seller but also influenced the political and moral debates over slavery as the country edged toward civil war. According to *Harper's*, by the 1850s women made up an astounding four-fifths of the reading public.

An emerging middle class, with its rising incomes, expectations, and living standards, made this new lifestyle possible. Starting in the eighteenth century, the economy had grown and diversified, giving an urban and market-oriented edge to what was still a predominantly agricultural country. American society had never been totally egalitarian—there were always rich and poor, even in the early colonial settlements—but the changes in the economy brought a more stratified class structure, especially in urban areas. At the center of this new system of exchange was cash: in the form of wages coming in for labor performed and goods sold, and money going out to buy a range of consumer goods and services that were no longer being produced in the household economy. Bostonian Abigail Lyman captured this shift perfectly when she exclaimed in 1797: "There is no way of living in this town without cash."

The story of domestic service, long the domain of women, exemplifies this growing class stratification. In the colonial and early Revolutionary eras, it was common for married women to have as "hired help" a local girl, often a neighbor's unmarried daughter, who came into the household on a casual basis to help out with household chores like cleaning, laundry, or cooking. In other words, she was basically the same class as her mistress. By the mid-nineteenth century, the gap between mistress and maid had dramatically widened. The women who took jobs as domestic servants were increasingly recent immigrants, especially from Ireland, and they often lived in as permanent but poorly paid employees. Critical to the rising housekeeping requirements of nineteenth-century households, domestic servants performed more specialized tasks while allowing middle-class families to flaunt their ability to afford such help. Heaven forbid that a mistress answer the door when a servant could do it.

And yet even the hiring of domestic servants did not free middle-class women from the demands of running a household. It merely redistributed the responsibilities to involve more supervision and less physical work. For example, middle-class women now devoted far more time to the instruction, moral or otherwise, of their children, a task that was rarely farmed out to servants. Well-brought-up children were now one of the main products of a middle-class family.

The labor that women performed in their homes in the early nineteenth century paralleled the growth of the large-scale economic development that historians call industrialization. As men increasingly defined themselves and their roles by working for wages outside the home, labor became synonymous with wages, and wages became synonymous with male gender roles. However, women's domestic labor, which was not paid, was not considered comparable work. Since the wages men earned were often barely enough to support a family, it was up to women to supply the difference, either by bringing in additional cash for the family coffers or by substituting their own labor for something that would otherwise involve an outlay of cash. Such economic activities could add as much as $150 a year to a family budget, a hefty subvention. These contributions were not some abstract ideology of domesticity: these were real women doing real work. And yet because women's domestic work was generally unpaid and undervalued, it was practically invisible.

The insufficiency of men's wages was especially problematic for working-class women and their families living in urban areas. Urban poverty was different from rural poverty, and working-class women struggled to scrounge needed resources for their families. In addition to taking in boarders (which brought in cash but also made more work for women), they might go out scavenging on the city streets with their children, looking for cast-off goods and food with which to feed the family. Women might take in piecework, earning pennies for work, such as sewing, that would later be consolidated in factories. Besides the precariousness of their existence, urban laboring women's lives lacked any sharp distinctions between public and private, with the urban neighborhood rather than the private home serving as the basis for working-class women's identity.

This focus on family and the household has implications beyond women's domestic roles. The economic contributions women made to their family survival in many ways allowed early capitalists to pay their male workers lower wages—and hence earn higher profits themselves. Thus housewives were central to the successful launching of industrialization. The home itself was also affected by the industrial transformation. New household technologies like central furnaces, cast-iron cookstoves, and sewing machines were beginning to reshape domestic chores and bring women's work more in line with the "time and task" routines characteristic of industrial labor.

Some women, mainly young farm girls from rural New England, played an even more direct role, flocking to the Lowell mills in the 1830s and 1840s. Women have always worked, but the Lowell experiment was the first large-scale industrial undertaking whose owners welcomed, indeed relied on (cheap) female labor to make their textile products. Adjusting to repetitive working conditions and twelve-hour days six days a week was a challenge, but in many ways the excitement of living on their own in company boardinghouses compensated for the poor conditions. "Don't I feel independent!" one mill worker wrote home to her sister in the 1840s. Kinship networks and cultural homogeneity also eased the transition to urban life. Confirming their sense of themselves as pioneers comparable to young men seeking their fortunes out West, Lowell mill girls contributed essays to the company-supported newspaper, the *Lowell Offering*, and later wrote books about their youthful experiences. Two of the best known are Lucy Larcom's *A New England Girlhood* (1889) and Harriet Hanson Robinson's *Loom and Spindle, or Life among the Early Mill Girls* (1898).

Alas, this heyday (if it ever was one) did not last. As early as the mid-1830s, female mill workers organized strikes to protest poor

Lowell mill girls

Sarah Hodgdon left her home in Rochester, New Hampshire, at the age of sixteen to work at the Merrimack Company factory in Lowell. Her reference to hiring a seat refers to the practice of "pew rent" common in urban churches at the time.

[June 1830]

Dear mother,

I take this opertunity to write to you to informe you that I have gone into the mill and like very well. I was here one week and three days before I went into the mill to work for my board. We boord t[o]gether. I like my boording place very well. I enjoy my health very well. I do not enjoy my mind so well as it is my desire to do so. I cant go to any meetings except I hear a seat therefore I have to stay home on that account. I desire you pay that it may not be said of me when I come home that I have sold my soul for the gay vanitys of this world. Give my love to my farther tell him not to forget me and to my dear sister and to my brothers and to my grammother tell her I do not forget her and to my Aunts and to all my enquiring friends....Dont fail writing. I bege you not to let this scrabling be seen.

Sarah Hodgdon

working conditions, long hours, and low pay; in the 1840s they formed labor unions. By then the owners of the mills had realized that New England farm girls were not the only cheap source of labor for their dramatically growing businesses: male and female immigrants from Ireland, then in the grip of a terrible famine, increasingly supplied the labor that ran the mills. And what of the Lowell mill girls? Even though they usually only worked in the mills for a few scant years, the experience had a lifelong impact. As a group, they tended to marry later and were more likely to stay in towns and cities rather than returning to rural farm life. Work outside the home was definitely a transformative experience for multiple generations of American women.

So, too, was participation in the gamut of religious, charitable, and reform societies that flourished in the first half of the nineteenth century, mainly in the Northeast but also in the recently settled Midwest. Even though women lacked access to traditional forms of political influence, such as the vote or participation in political parties, they were still very much involved in a range of political and cultural issues of their day. To put it another way, foregrounding women's reform and benevolent activities encourages a dramatic broadening of what constitutes political history.

The starting point for understanding this burst of reform is religion, specifically women's central roles as members of churches. As English novelist Frances Trollope observed after living in the new nation for several years in the late 1820s, never had she seen a country "where religion had so strong a hold upon the women, or a slighter hold upon the men." But this religious fervor ebbed and flowed, subject to bursts of revivalism (such as the Great Awakening, from the 1750s to the 1770s, and then the Second Great Awakening of the 1820s and 1830s) that brought new converts, male and especially female, into the Protestant fold. All this religiosity needed an outlet beyond just going to church on Sundays, and benevolent societies and voluntary associations flowed naturally from new conversions. By one estimate, at least 10 percent of all the adult white women in the Northeast participated in some form of benevolent reform in these years.

Women's benevolent work covered a range of initiatives and interests. Maternal societies brought women together in their shared role as mothers. For example, the Dorchester (Massachusetts) Maternal Association was founded in 1816 by members who were "aware of our highly responsible situation as Mothers & as professing Christians" and wanted to "commend our dear offspring to God." In contrast, moral reform societies hoped to hold men and women to a single high standard of purity, the standard adhered to by women. To that end such groups as the Boston Female Moral Reform Society attacked the sin of licentiousness, dedicating themselves to rescuing women who had "fallen" into prostitution. More controversially, these groups also aimed to publicize—and ostracize—the men who visited these prostitutes. All of this was done in the name of female moral superiority.

In essence, these benevolent associations were an attempt to use private charity to deal with many of the social problems that the state would later take on. Reformers tackled the problems of destitute widows and orphaned children, conditions for inmates in insane asylums and poorhouses, and public drunkenness. On more strictly religious grounds, voluntary associations supported missionary work abroad and promoted spiritual and personal improvement at home, especially temperance. These concerns were portrayed as especially well matched to women's heightened moral sensibilities, although women's rights activist Susan B. Anthony would have none of this, sneering: "Men like to see women pick up the drunken and falling. That *patching business* is 'woman's proper sphere.'" Anthony's dismissal notwithstanding, such benevolence provided access to activities more associated with the public than the private realm. Besides being numerous (as many as four hundred female moral reform societies existed in New York and New England by the 1840s), these groups were extremely sophisticated in their organization. Women ran meetings, organized outreach drives, raised and distributed vast sums of money, and publicized their activities, all while managing to keep up with their ongoing domestic responsibilities in the private sphere.

Until the 1830s almost all of women's benevolent and charitable work was in some way church related. (In contrast, men were free to join a range of civic, political, and religious associations.) At the

I Sell the Shadow to Support the Substance.

SOJOURNER TRUTH.

4. One of the *cartes de visite* (postcards) Sojourner Truth sold to raise money when she lectured—hence the caption "I Sell the Shadow to Support the Substance."

core of women's benevolence was allegiance to the ideal of moral suasion, that is, trying to convince individuals to change their erring ways through personal persuasion. But there were limits to how much society could be transformed in this manner, and by the 1840s and 1850s some women had concluded that "moral suasion is moral balderdash." Beware, however, of seeing an inevitable progression from moral reform and benevolence to more radical undertakings. Only a hearty and bold minority made that leap.

Two of the most important movements that captured their energies were antislavery and women's rights. Slavery was both a political and a moral question for the early republic, and it was only resolved (and then incompletely) by the Civil War of the 1860s. Starting in the 1830s, as slavery became more entrenched and profitable in the South, northern abolitionists began to challenge slavery as morally wrong in a democratic society. In 1831 William Lloyd Garrison founded the New England Anti-Slavery Society and welcomed women who shared his views, such as Quaker activist Lucretia Mott and former slave Sojourner Truth. Two early converts were Angelina and Sarah Grimké, sisters and southerners who turned against their heritage by embracing abolition. (Angelina would later marry fellow abolitionist Theodore Weld). Their presence caused consternation in the movement, however, when Sarah began to speak in public to mixed (or "promiscuous") audiences of both men and women, an act deemed too radical even to a committed bunch of radicals. But she would not be silenced, and soon other women added their public voices to the cause. This participation opened their eyes not just to the plight of the African American slave but eventually to women's plight as well. As abolitionist and women's rights activist Abby Kelley Foster put it eloquently, "We have good cause to be grateful to the slave. In striving to strike his irons off, we found most surely, that we were manacled ourselves."

Lucy Stone and Elizabeth Cady Stanton also came to women's rights through antislavery. Stone was one of the first women

Sojourner Truth

Sojourner Truth was born a slave in New York before the institution was abolished in that state in 1827. An itinerant preacher and abolitionist lecturer, Truth connected the struggles for women and slaves in this impassioned speech to an 1851 women's rights convention:

> I am a woman's rights [woman]. I have as much muscle as any man, and can do as much work as any man. I have plowed and reaped and husked and chopped and mowed, and can any man do more that that? I have heard much about the sexes being equal; I can carry as much as any man, and can eat as much too, if I can get it. I am as strong as any man that is now....

> I can't read, but I can hear. I have heard the Bible and have learned that Eve caused man to sin. Well, if woman upset the world, do give her a chance to set it right side up again....And how came Jesus into the world? Through God who created him and the woman who bore him. Man, where was your part?

to attend college (Oberlin class of 1847) and after graduation became an itinerant speaker for antislavery and women's rights. She would later marry abolitionist Henry Blackwell in a ceremony in which she refused to promise to obey her husband and pledged to keep her family name, hence the designation of women who followed her example as "Lucy Stoners." Elizabeth Cady grew up as the daughter of a judge in upstate New York, where sampling the law books in his library indelibly introduced her to discrimination against women in the law; when she married reformer Henry Stanton in 1840, they spent their honeymoon in London at a world antislavery conference. When women delegates were forced to sit in a balcony separately from the men, this slight was too much for Stanton and Mott, and together they vowed to hold a convention dedicated to women's rights. It took eight years before it came off, and when it did, it was in a tiny village in upstate New York, where the Stantons had settled with their growing family.

The Seneca Falls convention of 1848 was not, as is often asserted, the first conference ever held on the question of women's rights, but it has assumed a preeminent place in the history of feminism and women's rights. On two days in July, approximately three hundred people, including forty men, gathered in the local Methodist church in response to a call to discuss "the social, civil and religious condition of Woman" that had been drafted by Stanton, Mott, and Martha Coffin Wright at Stanton's kitchen table. (That table is now in the Smithsonian Institution.) Often these women are portrayed as simple housewives, but they were already savvy and experienced reformers, and they were determined not to back down, even when Henry Stanton threatened to leave town. Elizabeth Cady Stanton was their wordsmith, and she turned to the Declaration of Independence for inspiration, boldly restating its central concept in this unforgettable way: "All men and women are created equal."

The Declaration of Sentiments adopted at Seneca Falls presented eighteen instances of "repeated injuries and usurpation on the part of man toward woman," including the denial of the basic right of citizenship, the lack of married women's property rights, the exclusion of women from profitable employment, and the lack of access to education. All of these issues had been circulating separately for the past few decades, but the document pulled them together to make a compelling case for women as necessary subjects of a reform movement of their own. Eleven resolutions followed, all of which passed easily, with the exception of the call "to secure to themselves their sacred right to elective franchise," which just squeaked by. Why was woman suffrage so fraught? Because women voting alongside men would have been the ultimate challenge to the notion of politics and public life as men's sphere. Not until 1920, a full seventy-two years after Seneca Falls, would that right finally be achieved with the passage of the Nineteenth Amendment.

Absent from Seneca Falls was Susan B. Anthony, who was living in nearby Rochester and about to embark on a career as a temperance lecturer after a decade of teaching school. Soon dissatisfied with the secondary roles that women were expected to play in the temperance movement, she gravitated toward women's rights. In 1851 she met Elizabeth Cady Stanton, and the two formed one of the greatest political partnerships in women's history.

By then the notion of a separate women's sphere was clearly under assault. As a resolution at another early women's rights convention stated, "The proper sphere for all human beings is the largest and highest to which they are able to attain." Margaret Fuller, unquestionably the most prominent woman intellectual in antebellum America, was thinking along similar lines in her influential *Woman in the Nineteenth Century*, published in 1845: "We would have every arbitrary barrier thrown down. We would have every path laid open to Woman as freely as to Man." Thus did the political and intellectual ferment originally unleashed by the American Revolution continue to deepen and grow.

This ferment was actually a worldwide phenomenon, as a wave of uprisings and insurrections swept Europe in the revolutions of 1848. Margaret Fuller reported on these developments from Italy for Horace Greeley's *New-York Tribune*, making her America's first female war correspondent. Constituting what was arguably the first international women's movement, women on both sides of the Atlantic seized the moment to demand changes in women's status in society. In the Western Hemisphere, 1848 marked the end of the Mexican-American War and the signing of the Treaty of Guadalupe Hidalgo, by which Mexico ceded its vast northern territories stretching from Texas to California to the United States. It was not just at Seneca Falls, therefore, that new ideas about citizenship and democracy, as well as nationalism, were beginning to reshape American society, indeed the whole world.

Chapter 3

The challenges of citizenship, 1848–1920

Ida B. Wells was born a slave in Holly Springs, Mississippi, in 1862 during the upheavals of the Civil War and spent the rest of her life fighting for full citizenship, both as an African American and a woman. When a yellow fever epidemic killed her parents and a younger sibling in 1878, she dropped out of school and became a teacher to support her family. Seeking more opportunity, she relocated to Memphis, where she became a journalist. Her first brush with challenging discrimination came in 1883, when she was forcibly evicted from the "ladies" car on a Chesapeake & Ohio train and forced to relocate to the "colored" car. Indignant at her treatment, she sued the railroad company, claiming her right to ride in the ladies' car, for which she had purchased a ticket. The settlement she initially won from the railroad company was later overturned. Confirming the deteriorating climate for African American rights at the end of the nineteenth century, the Supreme Court upheld the practice of Jim Crow segregation in the 1896 case *Plessy v. Ferguson*.

Ida B. Wells is best known for her antilynching activism. Her epiphany occurred in 1892 in Memphis, where she had become part owner of a newspaper called the *Memphis Free Speech*. When three black men were lynched by a white mob, Wells exposed the real reason for the racial violence: the economic competition these successful black shopkeepers posed to white businessmen. As she later wrote in her autobiography, *Crusade for Justice*, "This is what opened my eyes to what lynching really was. An excuse to get rid of Negroes who were acquiring wealth and prosperity and thus keep the race terrorized and 'keep the nigger down.'" She did not stop there. Tackling head-on the claim that black men were lynched because they raped white women, Wells challenged the assumption that white woman never voluntarily engaged in sexual relations with black men. For such provocative statements, the office of her newspaper was trashed, and she was basically run out of town. Several years later she relocated to Chicago, where she married lawyer Ferdinand Barnett and had four children.

Antilynching was but one of the many crusades for justice that Ida B. Wells-Barnett (as she was now known) took on. In 1893 she publicly attacked the organizing committee at the World's Columbian Exhibition in Chicago for excluding the contributions of black women. In 1894 she challenged temperance leader Frances Willard for her racist statements about black men's moral character and demanded (without success) that the Woman's Christian Temperance Union (WCTU) make antilynching part of its broad reform agenda. In 1913 she organized one of the first black woman suffrage organizations, the Alpha Suffrage Club in Chicago, only to be told by white suffrage leader Alice Paul that she could not march in the suffrage parade timed to coincide with the inauguration of President Woodrow Wilson. Ida Wells-Barnett marched anyway, slipping into the Illinois delegation as the parade assembled and quietly but deliberately making her point that black women needed and deserved the vote just as much as white women.

Ida Wells-Barnett's lifelong activism offers a window on many of the pressing issues of American life from the Civil War through World War I, foremost of which was the struggle for African Americans to find political and economic justice after emancipation. Her career shows the new professional roles opening to women as journalists and business owners, and her temperance and suffrage work demonstrates the importance of women's organizations, as well as the potential tensions between black and white women in those groups. Finally, as a longtime resident of Chicago, she witnessed firsthand the impact of industrialization, immigration, and urbanization as those historical forces reshaped American life.

Gender and race in war and reconstruction

Two years into the Civil War, Lucy Buck observed: "We shall never any of us be the same as we have been." Buck was a white southerner, but she spoke for the multitudes of American women, few of whom escaped the four-year struggle of the Civil War untouched. And yet that impact differed by region and race, with southern women, black and white, bearing the heaviest burdens as their states became the battleground for the bloodiest war in American history.

Northern white women embraced the challenge of war patriotically. Many channeled their contributions through the U.S. Sanitary Commission, which despite its name was not a formal arm of the federal government but rather a huge voluntary association that took on the task of supplying the needs of the northern fighting force. Mainly propelled by women's volunteer efforts, the commission operated on an unprecedented national scale, including in the West. Women organized fundraising efforts called sanitary fairs, collected supplies and funds, and sewed and knitted for the benefit of Union soldiers and their kin. White women then transferred these newly acquired organizational skills into many of the institutional and reform movements they participated in for the rest of the nineteenth century. For example, Clara Barton drew on her wartime experiences to found the American Red Cross in 1881.

Although photographs of Civil War battlegrounds suggest an exclusively male terrain, women were not simply relegated to organizing charity fairs and knitting socks. Perhaps as many as three thousand women signed on as nurses under the supervision of Dorothea Dix, who followed in the footsteps of Crimean War pioneer Florence Nightingale. One of these eager nurses was Louisa May Alcott, whose beloved novel *Little Women* would be published in 1868. "I want new experiences, and am sure to get 'em if I go," she exclaimed, although she lasted less than a month before she contracted typhoid fever and had to return home. In addition to nurses, northern women also served as spies and soldiers, but only clandestinely. Far more prevalent were the camp followers who tagged along on the edges of the Union army, following husbands, brothers, and sons as they fought.

5. This photograph of the camp of the Thirty-First Pennsylvania Infantry near Washington, D.C., in 1862 confirms that women and children were part of the Civil War military experience.

Whereas just under half of the eligible northern men served in the Union army, closer to four-fifths of eligible southern men joined the Confederate ranks, leaving white women to constitute "a second front," literally running farms and plantations and supervising slaves while their men went off to war. Instead of seeing these responsibilities as an opportunity for expanded civic and familial roles (as many northern women did), southern white women often experienced these additional demands as an oppressive burden. Trained to depend on male protection, they were uncomfortable being left in charge on their own.

Managing slaves was especially difficult for elite southern women. Ensuring the compliance of a slave population depended on coercion and violence, tools women were often (although not always) loathe to deploy. And yet how else to keep their slaves working while war, with its tantalizing possibilities of freedom and liberation, was raging all around them? In addition, fears of being raped by male slaves, to say nothing of marauding Union soldiers, terrified women who already felt unprotected and vulnerable. Overwhelmed by these wartime challenges, many southern women wanted nothing more than to be rid of their slaves entirely. "You may give your Negroes away," wrote a Texas wife to her husband in 1864. "I cannot live with them another year alone."

The Civil War took a terrible toll: more than a million men killed or wounded. Each of those casualties left mothers, sisters, wives, and daughters; the lives of widows and the young women who would never have a chance to marry were especially upended. In the end, the union was saved and slavery abolished, but at a terrible human cost. The resolution of the conflict also offered a truly remarkable promise: a life of freedom for emancipated slaves.

Freedom came in fits and starts for enslaved African Americans, a population that included approximately 1.9 million women. Once the fighting began, some slaves simply took matters into their own hands and ran away, seeking refuge behind Union lines, although male slaves exercised this option far more than female. As the fighting moved deeper into the South, it became increasingly difficult to go about business as usual. Lincoln's Emancipation Proclamation of January 1863 applied only to slaves in territory still controlled by the Confederacy (and thus technically did not free a single slave), but it made the abolition of slavery a central objective of Union war policy; total emancipation came with the passage of the Thirteenth Amendment in 1865. But as the country's experience in Reconstruction and beyond showed, the challenges were just beginning.

The top priority for former slaves when the war ended was the reestablishment of family ties. Newspapers and circulars were full of announcements seeking out family members who had been scattered by wartime disruptions or sundered earlier by the domestic slave trade. Joining husbands and wives together in legal matrimony (something that had been denied under slavery) represented a powerful personal and political statement. Another top priority was education, especially literacy. The white northern schoolteachers, mainly of them New England "schoolmarms," who opened schools in areas like the Sea Islands in Georgia represented an early (if not sustained) attempt at interracial cooperation in the new South.

The transition from slavery to freedom was economic as well as familial, as newly emancipated African Americans learned the difficulties of coping in an economy based on waged labor. Unfortunately, the resources available to the Freedman's Bureau, the federal agency set up to aid newly freed slaves (who were essentially war refugees), never came close to the immense demand for those services. Despite hopes of individual land ownership at war's end, captured by the aspiration for "forty acres and a mule," most African American families found themselves landless and working for white landowners as agricultural

Yankee schoolteachers head to the South

Mary S. Battey was an unmarried Yankee schoolteacher who relocated to Andersonville, Georgia, after the war. Her report from December 1866 describes the opening of her school:

Our school begun—*in spite of threatening from the whites, and the consequent fear of the blacks*—with twenty-seven pupils, four only of whom could read, even the simplest words. At the end of six weeks, we have enrolled eight-five names, with *but fifteen unable to read*. In seven years teaching at the North, I have not seen a parallel to their appetite for learning, and their active progress. Whether this zeal will abate with time, is yet a question. I have a little fear that it may. Meanwhile it is well to "work while the day lasts." Their spirit *now* may be estimated somewhat, when I tell you that three walk a distance of four miles, each morning, to return after the five hours session. Several come three miles, and quite a number from two and two-and-a-half miles.

workers. Black women were an important component of these family units, but their labor was often not counted as such.

Sharecropping for a white owner was better than slavery, but not all that much, so many freed slaves relocated to southern cities such as Atlanta, Charleston, and New Orleans to try their luck there. In many ways black men had more options than black women, since under slavery they had sometimes learned a skilled trade like blacksmithing or carpentry. Black women seeking wages had only one option: domestic service. For example, in Atlanta in 1880, 98 percent of employed black women worked as domestic servants. The work was hard, but in contrast to the bondage of slavery, these domestic workers enjoyed definite advantages beyond just wages. When faced with a demanding white employer or her lecherous husband, the domestic servant could simply say: "I quit."

These postwar transitions occurred in a deteriorating racial climate. White southerners may have been defeated militarily, but their racial attitudes hardened. The 1866 founding of the Ku Klux Klan in Pulaski, Tennessee, was a direct response to black Americans asserting their new freedoms, especially in public life. Though the late 1860s saw some political breakthroughs as black men won elected office as Republicans in the overwhelmingly Democratic South, many of these gains evaporated when federal troops withdrew at the end of Reconstruction in 1877 and white southerners returned to power.

In this changing—and challenging—landscape, African American women exhibited a style of political activism that put notions of family and community at the forefront of their vision. Working through churches, voluntary organizations, schools, and other self-help vehicles, African American women aimed at improving conditions not just for individuals but also for the community at large. The goal of racial uplift was integrally connected to expanded roles for African American women. As educator Anna Julia Cooper argued in her 1892 book, *A Voice from the South*, "Only the BLACK WOMAN can say 'when and where I enter in the quiet, undisputed dignity of my womanhood, without violence and without suing or special patronage, then and there the whole NEGRO RACE ENTERS WITH ME.'"

This approach became even more necessary as Jim Crow restrictions were codified in the 1880s and 1890s, enforcing legal segregation of the races throughout the South and robbing black men of the political rights, including voting, that had been guaranteed by the Fourteenth and Fifteenth amendments. Undaunted, black communities persevered. An increase in residential segregation, for example, meant an opportunity to build autonomous black institutions, especially churches and schools, which African American women made part of their agenda of "lifting as we climb." In North Carolina after black men lost the vote, black women like Charlotte Hawkins Brown became the diplomats to the white community, lobbying for services and benefits and working to modify white attitudes by their dignified example. In the *Plessy* spirit of "separate but equal," the educational, employment, and charitable services available to blacks would never equal those available to whites, but in combination with the self-help efforts so prevalent in black communities, African American women's actions helped to make black life bearable as race relations plunged to their nadir by century's end.

New arrivals, working girls, and farm women

The United States is a land of immigrants, the textbooks tell us, a fact invariably illustrated by a photograph of Ellis Island or the Statue of Liberty in New York, where in the words of Emma Lazarus's immortal poem, generations of Europeans "yearning to breathe free" found their way to new lives in the new world. But New York and the East Coast were not the only points of entry. Angel Island in San Francisco Bay served as a comparable gateway for immigrants arriving from China, Japan, the Philippines, and other parts of eastern Asia to new lives in "Gum Sum" (Gold Mountain), the Chinese equivalent of the Promised Land. And for Mexicans, there was always the allure of "El Norte" across the Rio Grande River. Between 1860 and 1900, approximately one-quarter to one-third of the residents of the American West had been born in another country, a proportion even higher than in the East. Immigration is thus best understood within a bicoastal, multiborder perspective. Just as vital is putting gender at the center of the immigrant experience.

The Chinese offer a good starting point. Early Chinese migration to California, which started around the time of the Gold Rush of 1849 and expanded in the 1860s as the Chinese became the primary construction workers for western railroads, was predominantly male, a pattern often replicated in other immigrant groups. With the sex ratio hovering at about thirteen to one, Chinese men created a bachelor society centered around laundries and restaurants, with their sexual needs served by a small number of Chinese prostitutes who worked under near slavery conditions. In 1860 at least 85 percent of Chinese women in San Francisco were prostitutes, although the proportion had fallen to 28 percent in 1880 because Chinese women had moved into other jobs as domestic servants and garment workers. The Chinese faced not just virulent racial prejudice but discriminatory legislation designed to limit their entry into the United States, specifically the Chinese Exclusion Act of 1882. With so few Chinese women already here, this law made it extremely difficult for Chinese men to establish families, which seems to have been the point. Because the Chinese learned to exploit loopholes in the law, the Chinese sex ratio in San Francisco dropped to three and a half to one by 1920, allowing for the emergence of more stable family and community life.

If a Chinese man and a white woman wished to marry, they ran afoul of the miscegenation laws that predominated in the American West. While the best known examples of these laws were framed to prevent blacks and whites from marrying (generally black men and white women), their reach was in fact much broader. Less concerned with preventing interracial sex than upholding the principle of white property inheritance, these laws regulated the institution of marriage by making it difficult for nonwhite men to marry white women. Because the categories of race were more diverse in the multicultural West than in the black/white binary in the South, the sweep of miscegenation laws was similarly broader, encompassing the Chinese (sometimes called Mongolians), Filipinos (Malays), Japanese, and occasionally Native Americans. Unfortunately, the virulent racism and commitment to white supremacy behind the laws was nationwide.

The Chinese pattern of migration, where men came first to work at menial jobs in order to save enough to send for women to establish families, was common to many immigrant groups, especially Italians, Russians, and other Slavs. The one exception was the Irish, where women predominated from the start, a consequence of the grim prospects in their famished home country combined with a strong demand for domestic servants, an area where Irish girls predominated. So closely were the Irish associated with service that the name "Brigid" became practically synonymous with "maid."

The experiences of Irish immigrants demonstrate the push and pull factors that drove the decision to uproot oneself from one's home and journey to a new land in the hope of a better life. Conditions of poverty or limited opportunity in European countries such as Poland, Italy, and Russia (and for Jewish families, the added factor of bitter anti-Semitism) certainly pushed the decision to leave, but so did the pull factors in America, specifically the prospect of jobs in urban areas and, for farming immigrants, the prospect of land in the Midwest and American West.

The Civil War preserved the union, abolished slavery, and encouraged westward migration, but it also acted as an important spur to industrialization. Female wage labor was central to this surge. Whereas women made up 14 percent of the workforce in 1870, their percentage had grown to 20 percent by 1910, an increase in absolute numbers from 1.7 million to 7 million. The kinds of jobs women held were shaped not only by the structural needs of the economy and assumptions about what was suitable "women's work" but also by individual women seizing new opportunities created by broader economic change. Although the largest single occupational category for women remained domestic service, its predominance was declining as women seized the chance for any work other than the dreaded, dead-end job of servant. Most working women ended up in factories and sweatshops, especially in the sewing and textile trades. Higher status jobs, such as clerical and retail work or teaching, were usually reserved for the daughters of native-born Americans. Even though the hours were long and the pay sometimes lower than industrial work, the coveted white-collar jobs offered prospects for upward social mobility.

The typical working woman was young (usually between the ages of fourteen and twenty), single, lived in an urban area, and was the daughter of immigrants. She saw her work as temporary until she married and established a family of her own; very few married women worked for wages at this point. The one exception was in the African American community, where male wages were so low that married women needed to work in order to ensure family survival; a quarter of black married women worked in 1900, compared to 3 percent of comparable white women. But they had a far smaller range of options to choose from, mainly domestic service and agricultural work, since they were barred by prejudice from higher paying industrial jobs until well into the twentieth century.

Working conditions were harsh for the women (men, too) whose labor fueled American industrial growth. With few regulations or controls on working conditions except what the market would bear, the average work week for women was sixty hours over six days, with Sundays and part of Saturday afternoon off. In addition to harsh and often dangerous working conditions, seasonal layoffs and periodic unemployment added to the strain. Most working girls lived at home, often turning over their meager wages directly to their mothers. In their leisure time, urban working girls flocked to the new commercial entertainments such as dance halls, amusement parks, vaudeville theaters, and later movie houses. Dressed in their best clothes and on the lookout for nice chaps to treat them to food or drink, they experimented in new modes of sexuality and commercialized leisure, experiencing the combination of danger and pleasure that such encounters could bring. Needless to say, their immigrant mothers, housebound by domestic responsibilities and language barriers, often disapproved of their high-spirited daughters out on the town.

A tragic event that occurred in New York City in 1911 serves as a window on the conditions of working women's lives. On a Saturday afternoon in March, fire broke out at the Triangle Shirtwaist factory in Greenwich Village; when workers tried to flee, they found the exits had been locked by employers to prevent them from sneaking out from work early. To escape the raging inferno, many jumped or fell from the upper-story windows; their dead bodies soon littered the pavement. In all, 146 working women lost their lives that day. Just two years before the Triangle Fire, garment workers in New York City sweatshops had gone on a strike led by the International Ladies Garment Workers Union (ILGWU)—"the rising of the 20,000"—to protest working conditions. The strike lasted for three months and ended in some concessions, including a fifty-two-hour work week. Tragically, the owners of the Triangle Shirtwaist Company had refused to join the settlement. If they had, those 146 workers would not still have been working late on a Saturday afternoon when the fire broke out.

With the exception of unions such as the ILGWU, relations between the labor movement and working women were fraught. Male union leaders held highly traditional gender expectations and viewed women as temporary workers who belonged in the home; labor organizers' priority was protecting the wages of male workers so they could support their wives and children (the so-called family wage). Women had other ideas. Starting with Leonora Barry in the Knights of Labor in the 1880s and Mary Kenney in the American Federation of Labor in the 1890s, female labor organizers demonstrated that women workers would join unions and be an important part of the labor movement. Charismatic organizers such as Clara Lemlich, Rose Schneiderman, and Pauline Newman continued that fight in the early twentieth century, working to improve

Working in a glove factory

Agnes Nestor came from an Irish Catholic family and spent most of her working life in Chicago. This account, written around 1898, describes working in a glove factory. Fed up with these conditions, Nestor devoted the rest of her life to the International Glove Workers Union.

> The whistle blows at 7 a.m. but the piece workers have until 7.30 to come in to work. The penalty for coming late (after 7.30 a.m.) is the loss of a half day as the girls cannot then report to work until noon. This rule is enforced to induce the girls to come early but it often works a hardship on them when they are unavoidably delayed on account of the cars, etc. Stormy weather is the only excuse.

> All the work in the sewing department is piece work so the wages depend upon the speed of the operator....When I started in the trade and saw the girls working at that dreadful pace every minute, I wondered how they could keep up the speed. But it is not until you become one of them that you can understand. The younger girls are usually very anxious to operate a machine. I remember the first day that I sewed, making the heavy linings. The foreman came to me late in the day and asked how I liked the work. "Oh," I said, "I could never get tired of sewing on this machine." But he had seen too many girls "get tired," so he said "Remember those words a few years from now if you stay," and I have.

the terrible conditions of waged labor within established unions such as the ILGWU, as well as alongside elite reformers in organizations such as the National Consumers' League (founded in 1899) and the Women's Trade Union League (1903). It was an uphill fight. By 1920 fewer than 8 percent of women workers belonged to unions, despite making up 20 percent of the workforce.

6. These delegates to the Knights of Labor convention in 1886, including Elizabeth Rodgers with her two-week-old daughter, Lizzie, demonstrate working women's allegiance to the labor movement.

In thinking about issues of gender and work, it is helpful to flip the coin and look at the 80 percent of women who were not engaged in wage labor at the turn of the century. That, of course, does not mean that they did not work, and work hard, just that the work they did for their families was not counted as labor. In urban areas, the mothers of working girls, often recent immigrants themselves, were tasked with providing for their families under extremely difficult conditions created by poverty and recent arrival. Huddled in tenement housing without access to clean drinking water or indoor plumbing, wives learned to shop, cook, and barter to get what their families needed. With an increasing array of consumer goods available for purchase, there was never enough money to go around. Adapting Old World recipes and customs to New World realities, including different kinds of food, was a daily challenge. So was cleanliness in urban areas where most of the heat came from coal and water came from a pump out back. Disease often followed.

The challenges were just as acute for rural women in farming communities. Rural dwellers were the majority of Americans until 1920, but farm wives were an eclectic group: members of families who had been farming the land for generations; of recently emancipated slave families sharecropping in the rural South; of immigrant groups, such as Norwegians and Swedes, who created their own farming frontier in the Midwest; and of families who moved to the West in the transcontinental migration that started in the 1840s. All experienced moments of extreme loneliness and hard work as they worked alongside their husbands as part of the family unit. "Quit with a headache," confided an Arizona woman to her diary. "Done too much work." In addition to farm chores, rural women kept house, bore and raised children, fed their families and kept them clean all without the benefits of electricity or running water. Mechanization revolutionized farming starting in the late nineteenth century, but except for a sewing machine with a foot-treadle to provide power, technology mainly passed rural women by until well into the twentieth century.

Laundry was women's most onerous chore, an all-day affair (usually on Mondays) for which there was no remotely equivalent task for men. Since only one out of ten farms had electricity as late as the 1930s, hundreds of gallons of water had to be pumped by hand and then hauled to the house. The farm wife then heated the water on a woodstove that required constant tending, washed the clothes (often with harsh lye, since soap was too expensive), rinsed them, and wrung them out to dry. Then came another all-day task of ironing, which involved six- to seven-pound wedges of metal that had to be individually heated over a fire; a single shirt could take several irons. Southwest Texas farm women called them "sad irons."

To lessen the loneliness of farm life, especially on the Great Plains, where settlement was widely spaced out, farm women and their menfolk turned to collaborative efforts, both political and economic. These included farm cooperatives, which provided services and benefits to members who pooled their resources, as well as organizations like the Grange, a fraternal organization that welcomed women's participation. Rural women also participated in political movements, such as the Farmers' Alliance in the 1880s and the Populist Party in the 1890s. "What you farmers need to do," Populist orator Mary Elizabeth Lease memorably declared, "is to raise less corn and more *Hell!*"

Adventure and independence also beckoned. Case in point: the female homesteader. Taking advantage of a 1862 law that offered 160 acres of land to anyone—not just men—who kept up continual residence for five years while improving the land, a surprising number of women, mainly single, took this option: as many as 12 percent in a sample from Lamar, Colorado, and Douglas, Wyoming. And women were more tenacious at sticking it out than men, "proving up" their claims at a rate of 43 percent, versus 37 percent for men. Women's motives varied. Some were unmarried women on the lookout for a husband or a good investment. Widowed or divorced women might seek a way to provide for their families. But they all shared a sense of self-reliance and willingness to strike out in new directions.

Expanding horizons for educated women

In homesteading women we catch glimpses of what contemporaries were beginning to call "the New Woman." The New Woman of the 1890s was most readily distinguished by her dress. Instead of heavy corsets, yards of sweeping fabric, and elaborate millinery, she dressed comfortably in long dark skirts with simple white blouses called shirtwaists, a style made for movement and even athletic activity, such as riding a bicycle, the newest craze to sweep the country in that decade. As popularized by artist Charles Dana Gibson, the New Woman was a byproduct of the maturation of the industrial economy and the increasingly urban orientation of the country. As usual, many of these trends were more readily available to white, middle-class women than to recently arrived immigrants from Poland or Mexico or farm wives on the Plains, but there was a definite feeling of change in the air when it came to women's lives. As New Women entered the professions, tackled urban problems, and campaigned for birth control and woman suffrage, their lives, tentatively, began to prefigure the patterns that resemble women's lives today.

The middle-class home was changing as well, especially in urban areas, as the family completed a long-term shift from being a unit of production to one of consumption. Unlike their counterparts in rural America, urban women were the beneficiaries of technological developments, such as electricity, central heating, indoor plumbing, and kitchen appliances, that eased the burdens associated with housekeeping; urban women also enjoyed increased availability of consumer goods, including ready-to-wear clothing and processed food. The declining birthrate was one of the biggest changes in women's lives: over the course of the nineteenth century, the average number of births per woman dropped from seven in 1800 to three and a half in 1900. Women's life spans were also increasing, which meant they no longer spent their entire lives bearing and raising children. Much of this extra energy went into a flowering of civic engagement and municipal reform during the Progressive era, roughly 1890 to 1920.

The growth of higher education was an important precondition for women's new public engagement and one of the most far-reaching changes of the post–Civil War era. Fears about education making women unfit for roles as wives and mothers had a long history, and in 1873 a Harvard physician named Edward Clarke added a new concern: that using women's "limited energy" for the purpose of studying would harm the "female apparatus." In other words, seeking a college degree would damage women's reproductive capacity. This theory was quickly debunked by female physicians, who pointed out that it was possible to menstruate and think at the same time, but Clarke's fears lingered until the first generations of college graduates conclusively proved him wrong.

Women fought for access to education in different ways in each section of the country. In the West and Midwest the Morrill Land Grant Act of 1862 spurred the growth of land-grant colleges and state universities, which were mainly coeducational from the start, an important boost for women who aspired to learn alongside men. Higher education for women failed to flourish in the post–Civil War South, even for white women, but showed strong growth in the East. While some schools, such as Boston University and Cornell, opened their doors early to women, a more prevalent pattern was the establishment of women's colleges, such as the Seven Sisters, starting with Vassar in 1865, followed by Wellesley and Smith (1875), and Bryn Mawr (1884). On the West Coast, a Mount Holyoke graduate became the first president of all-female Mills College in 1885. Another pattern, again primarily in the East, was coordinate colleges, which paired women's instruction in separate institutions alongside the men's. The relationship forged between Harvard and Radcliffe College (founded in 1884) and Columbia and Barnard (1889) typified this pattern, as did the 1886 founding of Sophie Newcomb College as a coordinate to Tulane University in New Orleans.

Black women made access to education a high priority as part of their commitment to racial uplift. While a few schools, such as Oberlin, offered spots to black women (reformer Mary Church Terrell and educator Anna Julia Cooper both graduated from there in 1884, the only black members of their class), the prevailing racial climate meant that most breakthroughs occurred in all-black settings. Well-regarded colleges such as Fisk in Atlanta and Howard in Washington, D.C., were coeducational in large part because single-sex education was deemed too much of a luxury. One exception was Spelman, which started as a female seminary in Atlanta in the 1880s and became a women's college in 1925. Black women also attended vocational institutions such as Alabama's Tuskegee Institute or the Hampton Institute in Virginia for training in domestic and industrial arts. On graduation, many black women gravitated toward teaching, in large part because the segregated school systems that prevailed in the South (indeed, in the rest of the country) guaranteed that teaching positions, albeit with low pay and poor working conditions, were always available to them.

Education also played an important, if less liberatory, role in the history of Native American women. As written into law by the Dawes Severalty Act of 1887, the federal government divided reservation lands into individual family allotments and encouraged Native Americans to remake their societies and gender roles along a European model. To facilitate such changes, many Indian children were sent away to federally funded boarding schools, such as the Indian School in Carlisle, Pennsylvania, founded in 1879. At school, female students were expected to learn basic domestic and housewifery skills and conform to Anglo values and customs, including dressing in non-Indian clothing and speaking English. Being torn from tribal customs and familial networks was often a wrenching experience, as students found themselves educated to be part of a white society that had no place for them and increasingly out of step with the Native cultures from which they came.

By 1900, more than eighty-five thousand women were enrolled in colleges, making up 37 percent of all students; twenty years later, women made up almost 48 percent of students, an astounding rise. And yet these newly minted college graduates faced a daunting question: "After college, what?" For most, the choice remained marriage, coupled with a wide range of volunteer and civic activities. Yet a minority used their higher education as a stepping-stone to a career, embracing professional work as an attractive alternative to marriage. Very often these pioneering professional women chose to share their lives with other like-minded women in relationships that provided emotional support and financial security. The term "Boston marriage" described the prevalence of these deeply felt female friendships.

A Native American surveys Indian education

Zitkala-Sä, or Gertrude Simmon Bonnin, a Yankton Sioux from South Dakota, was educated at a Quaker missionary school and Earlham College and then taught for two years at the Indian School in Carlisle, Pennsylvania. Deeply disillusioned with the education offered to Native Americans, she wrote about her experiences in a series of *Atlantic Monthly* essays in 1900 and later became a leader in the Indian Reform movement.

Now, as I look back upon the recent past, I see it from a distance, as a whole. I remember how, from morning till evening, many specimens of civilized peoples visited the Indian school. The city folks with canes and eyeglasses, the countrymen with sunburnt cheeks and clumsy feet, forgot their relative social ranks in an ignorant curiosity. Both sorts of these Christian palefaces were alike astounded at seeing the children of savage warriors so docile and industrious.

As answers to their shallow inquiries they received the students' sample work to look upon. Examining the neatly figured pages, and gazing upon the Indian girls and boys bending over their books, the white visitors walked out of the schoolhouse well satisfied: they were educating the children of the red man! ...

In this fashion many have passed idly through the Indian schools during the last decade, afterward to boast of their charity to the North American Indian. But few there are who have paused to question whether real life or long-lasting death lies beneath this semblance of civilization.

The range of professional options open to educated women at the end of the nineteenth century never matched those available to men, nor did their pay. Teaching and librarianship continued to draw large numbers of trained women, as did newer professions such as nursing, social work, and home economics. Women made up a surprisingly high percentage of doctors at the turn of the century but much lower proportions in law and business. Women scientists faced an especially daunting task, often consigned to lesser ranks with little hope of advancement either in academe or industry. A professorship at a women's college offered one viable career path.

The settlement house movement also drew on the talents of educated women. Jane Addams and Ellen Gates Starr founded Hull House in Chicago in 1889, and soon settlement houses popped up in cities around the country. Settlement houses functioned as combinations of community centers and social service providers, offering recreational and educational services such as day care, poetry readings, literacy classes, and health and hygiene programs to the inhabitants of the poor neighborhoods in which they were located. These services were provided by settlement house residents drawn from the ranks of newly educated women (and a few men) who lived together communally in an atmosphere that resembled a college dorm. Settlement houses were a win-win situation: they provided crucial services to poverty-stricken neighborhoods whose needs were not being addressed by city and state governments, and they provided a collegial, family-like living situation for their residents. For her stewardship of Hull House, Jane Addams became one of the Progressive era's most celebrated women.

Just four years after the founding of Hull House, the World's Columbian Exposition opened in Chicago. A chance to trumpet the industrial, economic, and cultural strength of the United States on the threshold of becoming a world power, the Chicago World's Fair also showcased the important roles that women were playing in civic life. For example, the Woman's Building featured female contributions to culture, art, and history in a monumental structure designed by architect Sophia Hayden and overseen by a

Board of Lady Managers, headed by prominent Chicago clubwoman Bertha Honoré Palmer. The refusal of the Woman's Building board to acknowledge black women's contributions drew the ire of Ida B. Wells, but that did not keep it from being one of the fair's most popular destinations.

Efforts like the Woman's Building drew on the energies and organizational know-how of the women's club movement. As epitomized by the establishment of the General Federation of Women's Clubs in 1890, clubwomen came together in their communities to discuss causes and concerns of interest to them as civic-minded women. While many women's clubs served social functions for an emerging white middle-class elite, they could also be pathways into wider civic engagement. As the Federation's president, Sarah Platt Decker, said forthrightly in 1904, "Dante is dead. He has been dead for centuries, and I think it is time we dropped the study of the Inferno and turned the attention to our own."

Black women also felt the call of civic engagement through the club movement and settlement houses, but due to the prevailing racism at the time, their efforts were generally conducted separately from those of white women. Mary Church Terrell served as the first president of the National Association of Colored Women, which was incorporated in 1896 with one hundred member organizations; by 1914, the Association represented fifty thousand women in one thousand clubs. Often clubs came into existence to work for educational and social welfare goals in local communities, driven by an emphasis on race pride accompanied by strong leadership roles for African American women. The founding of Neighborhood House in Atlanta in 1913 by Lugenia Burns Hope and other local clubwomen reflects this dual focus on racial uplift and female activism. A similar impulse motivated the establishment of the first major Chinese women's club—the Chinese Women's Jeleab [Self-Reliance] Association—in San Francisco in 1913.

As these examples of women's activism suggest, women played prominent roles in a wide range of late nineteenth- and early twentieth-century reform initiatives. Much of the impetus for this activism came from women's identities as wives and mothers. How could women provide healthful and safe lives for their families, they argued, if city drinking water was contaminated, garbage filled the streets, and tuberculosis was rampant? More broadly, in what progressive reformer Mary Ritter Beard tagged municipal housekeeping, women reformers pressured city governments to provide city services as a way of protecting the health and well-being of all residents.

There was something larger going on here, and it involved women's changing relationship to the state. In a country known for unfettered capitalism and laissez-faire individualism, the role of the federal government and its state and local equivalents was fairly limited throughout most of the nineteenth century. Women reformers were among the first to realize that the enormous problems that American society faced at the end of the nineteenth century—linked to its rapid industrialization, the explosive growth of its cities, and the arrival of millions of new immigrants—called for coordinated and collaborative responses far beyond the resources of individuals. Who had those resources? The state. And so began a campaign, central to Progressive era reform, to expand the social welfare services of local, state, and federal governments. What had long been women's province through voluntary associations and charitable institutions was increasingly defined as a proper scope for public policy.

This new emphasis, and the rewards it reaped, are best seen in the field of child welfare. A generation of social reformers, many of them settlement house veterans, identified a broad range of issues demanding state intervention, such as the scourge of child labor, the dramatically high rates of infant mortality, and the lack of recreational and play spaces. These problems in turn were related to a host of others: tenement housing, long hours and low pay for women workers, industrial accidents, poor schools, and unsafe food products. Working together with women's clubs and other political and voluntary associations, such as the Women's Trade Union League and the National Consumers' League, determined Progressive women won results from recalcitrant elected and appointed officials.

One of the most concrete victories was the creation of the U.S. Children's Bureau in 1912, headed by Hull House alumna Julia Lathrop and tasked with investigating and improving the conditions of children's lives. Lillian Wald of the Henry Street Settlement, a pioneering organization in New York City that brought nursing services to the city's poor, thought it was about time. Referring to a federal study of the boll weevil, which was decimating the southern cotton crop, Wald observed pointedly, "If the Government can have a department to take such an interest in what is happening to the cotton crop, why can't it have a bureau to look after the nation's child crop?" One important byproduct was that professionally trained women found employment opportunities in government as it expanded its purview to include issues of vital concern to the nation's Progressive-minded women. The irony is that women did all this without the vote.

The final push for suffrage

In the end it took three generations to win the vote for American women. Pioneers such as Elizabeth Cady Stanton, Susan B. Anthony, and Lucy Stone dominated the movement throughout much of the nineteenth century. A second generation, represented by Carrie Chapman Catt and Anna Howard Shaw, entered the scene in the 1890s and early 1900s, when suffrage was on the verge of breaking out of the doldrums. And a third generation, epitomized by the indomitable Alice Paul, helped push it over the top with militant tactics in its final decade.

The original women's rights movement and abolitionism went hand in hand in the 1850s, and during the Civil War, leaders consciously set aside their activist agenda to build support for the Union cause. When the war ended, the old coalition linking race and gender split irrevocably over constitutional amendments intended to guarantee the political rights of recently freed slaves. Why? Because the wording of the Fourteenth Amendment introduced "male" into the Constitution in the context of voting rights. More broadly, the dispute was over who had priority: African American men or white women, who also wanted to be included in the post–Civil War expansion of political liberties. The nod went to African Americans, but at the cost of a unified women's rights movement, which split into two branches in 1869: the American Woman Suffrage Association (AWSA), headed by Lucy Stone and based in Boston, which supported what Wendell Phillips called "the Negro's Hour," and the National Woman Suffrage Association (NWSA), spearheaded by Susan B. Anthony and Elizabeth Cady Stanton out of New York, which did not.

Without a base of popular support, there was plenty of work for two groups to do. The AWSA founded the *Woman's Journal* in 1870, later edited by Alice Stone Blackwell (daughter of Lucy and Henry), which brought the powerful ideas and personalities of the movement to subscribers across the nation. Susan B. Anthony managed to register and vote in her hometown of Rochester, New York, in 1872 ("Well I have been & gone & done!! Positively voted the Republican ticket") but was quickly convicted of violating federal voting laws. A court challenge initiated by Missouri suffragist Virginia Minor claiming that women already had the right to vote because of general language of citizenship in the Constitution was shot down unanimously by the Supreme Court in *Minor v. Happersett* (1875). Failure to win legal redress forced suffragists back into the political arena.

The case of Utah shows how complicated suffrage politics could be. The Mormon leaders who dominated Utah politics supported the vote for women, but because of their controversial practice of plural marriage, conservative suffragists like Lucy Stone and the AWSA would have nothing to do with them. Elizabeth Cady Stanton and Susan B. Anthony had no such qualms: Mormons' allegiance to suffrage was more than enough to make them good allies. (This capacious approach had gotten NWSA into trouble before, specifically with an eccentric reformer named George Train, who funded their journal *Revolution* and then left them with a huge debt.) Caught in the middle were Utah's women, many of whom were strong suffrage supporters. When Utah gained territorial status in 1870 it enacted woman suffrage, but that was stripped away by Congress in 1887 because of polygamy. Finally in 1896, when Mormon leaders disavowed the practice as part of the price of statehood, the vote was restored.

The Utah story makes a broader point: the earliest victories came from Western states (Colorado, Utah, Idaho, and Wyoming) rather than the more conservative East or South. At the national level, passions and egos kept NWSA and AWSA far apart, but on the ground in localities far from Boston or New York, the differences between the rival groups were less clear. And while the names most associated with the national movement are those of eastern women, the West supplied a distinguished list of activists for the cause: Abigail Scott Duniway in Oregon, Jeannette Rankin in Montana, Emmeline B. Wells in Utah, Emma Smith DeVoe in Washington, and Caroline Severance and Maud Younger in California, among others.

Woman suffrage also had an interesting comrade in arms in these years: the temperance movement, then at the height of its influence. Under the charismatic leadership of Frances Willard from 1879 until her death in 1898, the WCTU moved far beyond a single-issue approach to temperance by embracing Willard's mandate to "Do Everything." Doing everything include supporting woman suffrage, which the WCTU endorsed in 1884.

In 1890 the two rival factions reunited as the National American Woman Suffrage Association (NAWSA). By this point the arguments for suffrage were undergoing a subtle but important shift. Whereas the early demands had rested on questions of equality and citizenship—women's right to vote as citizens—by the 1890s the justification turned more to what women would do with the vote, an argument from expediency. Suffragists also played up women's supposed moral superiority. At the same time, the focus of the movement narrowed from a broad definition of women's rights (including property laws, divorce, economic rights, and dress reform) to a single-minded focus on the vote.

By the 1890s the suffrage movement was part and parcel of the larger Progressive era reform movement. As civic-minded women dramatically increased their involvement in public life and civic affairs, their contributions strengthened the case for giving women the vote. But just as Progressive reform never really took hold in the South, the movement for suffrage also foundered in that region, caught up on the complicated question of race. If women won the vote, would black women be enfranchised, even though black men were now effectively disenfranchised by a variety of tools such as poll taxes, property requirements, and literacy tests? Alternatively, should suffragists argue that white women's votes would counteract the potential political power of African Americans? As Ida B. Wells-Barnett found, a pattern of deeply ingrained racism—a definite blind spot—clearly animated suffrage activism, as it did most Progressive era reform.

As late as 1909, only four states had given women the vote. The original suffrage leaders had died off—Lucy Stone in 1893, Elizabeth Cady Stanton in 1902, and Susan B. Anthony in 1906. New NAWSA leaders, such as Anna Howard Shaw and Carrie Chapman Catt, proved unable to break the stalemate. Over the next ten years, the momentum dramatically shifted. New tactics, new recruits, and a more supportive political climate paved the way for the final push to victory. Most prominent was a new focus on spectacle, which literally took the battle to the streets in the form of suffrage parades, open-air meetings, and the hawking of suffrage newspapers on street corners. The movement also branched out into immigrant and working-class communities to mobilize support. Suddenly male voters started taking notice: Washington adopted suffrage in 1910, followed by California in 1911 and Kansas in 1912. Note that success still lagged in the conservative East, and certainly the South. Not until 1917 did New York state join the trend.

As a consequence of these suffrage victories, many women were actually voting in local, state, and federal elections well before the passage of the Nineteenth Amendment in 1920. Women voters played especially key roles in western politics and in the 1912 third-party campaign of Theodore Roosevelt on the Progressive Party ticket. Symbolic of women's prominence in Progressive Party leadership, Frances Kellor headed the publicity and research committee, and Jane Addams, who put Roosevelt's name in nomination, was considered a possible cabinet choice.

As suffrage picked up momentum, so did other movements relating to women. One of the most pressing issues was birth control, which was illegal throughout most of the United States. Into that fray stepped a young public health nurse named Margaret Sanger, who opened the first birth control clinic in the Brownsville section of New York in 1916—and was promptly arrested. Sanger would remain in the forefront of reproductive rights for the next forty years.

Other activists positioned themselves far to the left of suffrage. Emma Goldman preached anarchism and socialism, "rebel girl" Elizabeth Gurley Flynn led general strikes in Paterson, New Jersey, and Lawrence, Massachusetts, and Charlotte Perkins Gilman challenged the theoretical underpinnings of marriage. Heterodoxy, a club for women "who did things, and did them openly," convened in New York's Greenwich Village in 1912, a harbinger of a strange new thing called feminism. (The term was first introduced in the United States at a mass meeting in 1914.) Staking out their turf, a witty supporter quipped, "All feminists are suffragists, but not all suffragists are feminists."

By now suffrage, temperance, and feminist activism were all part of vibrant international networks, linking activists across national borders and promoting a rich circulation of ideas and strategies, just as transnational abolitionism and women's rights had done in the 1830s and 1840s. In the 1880s the World's Woman's Christian Temperance Union took the lead, pursuing political equality for women in places such as New Zealand, Australia, and South Africa. In the 1890s and early 1900s, prodded by the advocacy of German socialist Clara Zetkin, the Second Socialist International made woman suffrage and women's political equality a central demand. In a separate development, the establishment of the International Woman Suffrage Association in 1904 fed the growth of the woman suffrage movement worldwide and facilitated the emergence of militant suffragism.

This international cross-fertilization is best seen in the impact of the suffrage militancy pioneered in England by the Women's Social and Political Union, led by Emmeline Pankhurst and her daughters Christabel and Sylvia. Their tactics were far more confrontational than petitions and parades: they involved breaking windows, setting bombs, attempted arson, and even (in the case of Emily Davison) running out onto a race course and being trampled to death, all to bring attention to the cause. In return, the militants were arrested and forcibly fed when they went on hunger strikes.

Alice Paul, a young Quaker from New Jersey, fell under the sway of the Pankhursts when she was studying abroad. Returning to the United States in 1911, Paul was determined to shake things up, and she most certainly did. First she organized a huge parade in Washington in 1913 to compete with President Woodrow Wilson's inauguration. (This was the parade Ida B. Wells-Barnett had to sneak into in order to march.) Four years later, when Wilson still refused to support suffrage, Paul and members of the National Woman's Party began picketing the White House, an unprecedented act of civil disobedience. Like their British sisters, they were arrested and thrown in jail; when they, too, went on hunger strikes, they were forcibly fed. The spectacle of elite white women willing to risk death for the cause garnered enormous publicity, and no small amount of sympathy, for the militants. Rose Winslow, who went on a hunger strike after being arrested, put it forcefully: "God knows we don't want other women ever to have to do this over again."

Carrie Chapman Catt, president of NAWSA, pointedly distanced her organization from the militants and concentrated, starting in 1917, on what she called her "Winning Plan." The new emphasis downplayed the costly and time-consuming focus on winning referenda state by state in favor of a massive lobbying effort behind a federal amendment. The suffrage amendment passed the House in 1918 and the Senate in 1919, and then was sent to the states for ratification. This was no easy task, but on August 26, 1920,

7. **National Woman's Party protesters representing colleges as diverse as Vassar and the University of Missouri picket the White House in 1918, demanding that President Woodrow Wilson support votes for women.**

Tennessee put the amendment over the top. The seventy-two-year struggle was finally over.

Many factors help to explain both the length of the struggle and its final success. What began as a truly radical demand in 1848 had become much less threatening by the early twentieth century, when the boundaries of women's lives stretched much farther than the home. Still, political machines, liquor interests, and religious groups such as the Catholic Church were formidable enemies, as was an organized antisuffrage movement, including many women who inconveniently announced they did not need or want the vote. To counteract that potent opposition, suffragists drew on the wealth of experience they had amassed in women's clubs, voluntary associations, charitable organizations, and political parties. Even the schisms that divided the movement—between AWSA and NWSA in the 1870s and 1880s and between NAWSA and the Woman's Party in the 1910s—arguably helped build momentum, each side drawing supporters who might have shunned the other. In the end what made the suffrage movement so powerful—and ultimately guaranteed its success—was that it brought together a diverse range of individuals and organizations in a broad coalition dedicated to a common goal.

Women's home front contributions during World War I finally tipped the balance, even though suffrage leaders were deeply divided over America's entry. The National Woman's Party opposed the war and defiantly continued to picket the White House, carrying placards that provocatively countered Wilson's campaign pledge to "make the world safe for democracy" with a call to "make the country safe for democracy." In contrast, Carrie Chapman Catt threw the entire weight of the much larger NAWSA behind the war effort. These patriotic efforts, as well as those by nonsuffrage women's groups, led many politicians and ordinary citizens to conclude that women deserved the vote.

World War I was a watershed beyond just woman suffrage. African Americans, dismayed by the worsening racial climate in southern states, were drawn by opportunities, wartime and other, in northern cities. Thus began the Great Migration, which between 1914 and 1920 saw five hundred thousand African Americans, half of them women, leave the South for Chicago, Los Angeles, New York, and beyond. With that dispersal, questions of race, instead of just being confined to the South, began to emerge as national concerns. Indeed, American race relations eventually became part of international affairs, as the United States became a world power in the aftermath of Europe's most destructive war to date.

In the meantime, on Election Day, 1920, some 26 million women were eligible to go to the polls, confirmation of their new status as the political equals of men. Of course such sentiments were

The Great Migration

More than any other city, Chicago represented the "promised land" for southern female African American migrants. Before heading North, many asked the *Chicago Defender*, the militantly problack newspaper founded in 1905, for help.

New Orleans, La. May 7, 1917.

Gentlemen: I read Defender every week and see so much good youre doing for the southern people & would like to know if you do the same for me as I am thinking of coming to Chicago about the first of June, and wants a position. I have very fine references if needed. I am a widow of 28. No children, not a relative living and I can do first class work as house maid and dining room or care for invalid ladies. I am honest and neat and refined with a fairly good education. I would like a position where I could live on places because its very trying for a good girl to be out in a large city by self among strangers is why I would like a good home with good people. Trusting to hear from you.

most likely held by privileged white middle-class women, but black women and working-class women had also campaigned hard for the vote. While in hindsight the vote may seem a fairly minor reform, women at the time, beneficiaries of the sense of camaraderie and shared partnership characterized this unique political movement, had a far different perspective.

The passage of the Nineteenth Amendment marked a significant milestone in another way. Politically active women no longer had a common goal to rally around, as Anna Howard Shaw warned Missouri suffragist Emily Newell Blair: "I am sorry for you young women who have to carry on the work in the next ten years, for suffrage was a symbol and you have lost your symbol." Luckily for Blair and other suffrage veterans, the postsuffrage era would bring just as many opportunities as challenges as women moved resolutely into the modern era.

Chapter 4
Modern American women, 1920 to the present

In a short book called *It's Up to the Women*, published in 1933, Eleanor Roosevelt challenged America's female citizens to pull the country through the gravest economic crisis it had ever faced: "The women know that life must go on and that the needs of life must be met and it is their courage and determination which, time and again, have pulled us through worse crises than the present one." When President Franklin D. Roosevelt took office in March, one-quarter of the country was unemployed, and the economy had ground to a halt. The banks were closed, and hunger stalked the cities and the countryside alike. As FDR took unprecedented steps to address the economic crisis and its underlying causes, Eleanor was at his side, always pushing him to do more. She truly served as the conscience of the New Deal.

Eleanor Roosevelt was perhaps the most influential and admired American woman of the twentieth century, but her early life hardly predicted such an outcome. Born into an elite family in New York in 1884, as a child she felt ugly compared to her beautiful socialite mother and desperately in need of affection from her alcoholic father. Orphaned at age ten, she and her younger brother were shuttled among various relatives. Her life began to open up when she was sent abroad to school in England. At Allenswood, a preparatory school run by a charismatic Frenchwoman named Marie Souvestre, Eleanor cultivated her intellectual aspirations and discovered her leadership abilities. College was not an option for most women of her class background, so she reluctantly "came out" into society as an eighteen-year-old, in effect putting herself on the marriage market. In 1905 she married Franklin Delano Roosevelt, her distant cousin from the Hyde Park branch of the family; her uncle Theodore, then president of the United States, gave the bride away. Eleanor Roosevelt bore six children over the next ten years, five of whom survived infancy, and seemed destined for a life of conventional upper-class womanhood.

It did not turn out that way. In 1910 her husband entered politics in Albany, and she found to her great surprise that she loved the rough-and-tumble of political life. Her horizons broadened further as she followed her husband to Washington when he joined the administration of President Woodrow Wilson in 1913. Despite her husband's infidelity with her social secretary during World War I and his being stricken with polio in 1921, she and Franklin forged a strong personal and political partnership. He reentered political life, and she became active in social reform circles and Democratic politics. When the Roosevelts took up residence at the White House in 1933, she was already a political force in her own right, a role she played throughout the Depression and war years and after her husband's death in 1945, when she became an advocate for international understanding in the postwar world. One of her last public roles was to chair the President's Commission on the Status of Women in 1961, which helped encourage the revival of feminism in the decades to come. A model of public-spirited womanhood that still resonates today, Eleanor Roosevelt represents the enormous contributions modern women made to American life in the years after suffrage was won.

New dilemmas for modern women

"The world broke in two in 1922 or thereabouts," observed writer Willa Cather. She was not specifically referring to women's new roles as citizens and voters but more broadly to changes in American life that marked the emergence of a mass, predominantly urban culture. Automobiles, movies, radio, telephones, mass-circulation magazines, brand names, and chain stores bound Americans together in an interlocking web of shared national experience, as did a new emphasis on consumption, leisure, and self-realization. Women were at the center of many of these broader developments, although modernity's benefits remained most accessible to the white middle class.

The flapper symbolized the new roles for women. With her bobbed hair and slim, boyish figure (achieved by the new fad of dieting), brazenly wearing makeup and smoking cigarettes in public, the flapper symbolized the personal freedom trumpeted by the emerging mass culture, including a freer approach to relationships with the opposite sex. True, the goal was still marriage, but young women had much more freedom once chaperonage went the way of horse-drawn carriages. Men could be friends and buddies, not just future husbands, reflecting a new sociability in modern life.

These new freedoms caused conflict and confusion as well as liberation, especially among parents shocked at the new liberties being taken by what the movies dubbed "our dancing daughters." And this conflict was not just limited to the white middle class. Adolescent Mexican American girls embraced the new flapper styles of dress, appearance, and unchaperoned behavior, much to the horror of their more conservative parents, who wanted to keep them under stricter control. And young Japanese American girls of the Nisei (second) generation turned to advice columnists such as "Dear Deidre" (in real life a journalist named Mary Oyama) for help in navigating such new challenges as interracial dating and conflicts between parental expectations about arranged marriages and marrying for love.

Many of these young girls got their modern ideas from the movies, one of the most powerful forms of mass culture and an enormously influential force in shaping women's aspirations from the 1920s on. From watching movies young women learned how to style their hair, covet the latest fashions, even how to act around men, including the proper way to kiss and make out. Hollywood and the growing film industry attracted star-struck teenagers who headed out to California in the hope of becoming movie stars. Barring that, lots of roles were available behind the cameras as screenwriters, script girls, and wardrobe managers. Hollywood actresses, such as Clara Bow, Gloria Swanson, Theda Bara, and Mary Pickford, became some of the most well-known women of their era. Successful, too: Pickford was one of the four founders of the Universal Artists studio.

While most of the images on the screen were of white women, there were some exceptions. Lupe Vélez and Dolores del Rio found success, but only by conforming to stereotypes about Latin women: del Rio presented herself as an exotic foreigner, and Vélez pitched herself as a "red hot tamale." African American actresses in the 1920s and 1930s, such as Hattie McDaniel, usually found the only roles available on screen were as maids and domestics. When criticized for playing into racial stereotypes, McDaniel pointedly replied, "It's better to get $7,000 a week for playing a servant than $7.00 a week for being one."

Affirmations of African American racial pride and cultural identity found more acceptance outside Hollywood. The Harlem Renaissance, an artistic movement of young writers and artists who championed racial awareness in the midst of white society, showcased the talents of writers Zora Neale Hurston, Jessie Fauset, and Nella Larsen. And befitting a decade that is often referred to as the Jazz Age, jazz and blues singers, such as Bessie

Smith, Ida Cox, and Ma Rainey, boldly sang about women's power and sexuality in songs such as "One Hour Mamma," which demanded that the singer's male lover slow down and pay attention to her sexual needs.

The Harlem Renaissance

Zora Neale Hurston became involved in the Harlem Renaissance while studying anthropology at Barnard College in the 1920s. In this 1928 essay, she exhibits both race pride and a sense of being beyond race, a mindset shared by other black writers at the time.

> At certain times I have no race, I am me. When I set my hat at a certain angle and saunter down Seventh Avenue, Harlem City, feeling as snooty as the lions in front of the Forty Second Street Library, for instance. So far as my feelings are concerned, Peggy Hopkins Joyce on the Boule Mich with her gorgeous raiment, stately carriage, knees knocking together in a most aristocratic manner, has nothing on me. The cosmic Zora emerges. I belong to no race nor time. I am the eternal feminine with its string of beads.
>
> I have no separate feeling about being an American citizen and colored. I am merely a fragment of the Great Soul that surges within the boundaries. My country, right or wrong.
>
> Sometimes, I feel discriminated against, but it does not make me angry. It merely astonishes me. How can they deny themselves the pleasure of my company? It's beyond me.

Despite the lure of becoming a movie star or a jazz singer, most young women ended up not with glamorous careers but as wives and mothers. But marriage, too, was changing. Men were still heads of households and primary breadwinners, but a higher value was placed on the wife's contributions to family life, especially her role in raising children. And there was definitely a higher recognition of women's sexual needs, as long as they were safely confined within marriage. In part because of the popularization of the ideas of Sigmund Freud, the new marital ideal involved satisfying sexual expression for both husbands and wives. The increasing availability and acceptance of birth control, which allowed women to enjoy sexual relations for purposes other than procreation, encouraged this trend.

In an economy increasingly based on consumption, women played vital roles as the primary consumers of the household goods so lavishly advertised in the decade's magazines and newspapers. But all the new appliances did not necessarily free women from domestic chores: a new vacuum cleaner or washing machine could actually create more work if the husband expected a clean shirt every day and the house was now vacuumed daily instead of swept once a week. And of course these new gadgets and appliances were useful only to households that had the disposable income to pay for them, plus electricity to run them, conditions that left out much of rural America.

As they had been doing since the nineteenth century, women continued to expand their activities beyond the home in volunteer activities and politics. Compared with the organized vitality of the suffrage movement, especially in its last decade, women's activism in the 1920s was more diffuse. But it would be wrong to conclude that suffrage did not matter or that women beat a hasty retreat from politics after 1920. Women played a prominent role in the passage of the Sheppard-Towner Federal Maternity and Infancy Act of 1921, the nation's first federally funded public health campaign. Women moved into the Democratic and Republican parties, often joining separate women's auxiliaries or clubs, although they quickly found that most political decisions were still made by men in smoke-filled rooms. In their new roles as citizens, women joined the League of Women Voters or participated in the Women's Joint Congressional Committee, a coalition of ten major women's organizations. While former suffragists continued to be associated with social reform, conservative women came together in patriotic or right-wing groups such as the Women Sentinels of the Republic, the Daughters of the American Revolution, and the women's wing of the Ku Klux Klan, which enrolled as many as five hundred thousand women in the 1920s.

The most divisive issue for politically active women in the postsuffrage era was the Equal Rights Amendment. This may seem surprising: why would women be opposed to equal rights? The controversy came down to the value of protective legislation that had been enacted during the Progressive era to regulate the hours and working conditions of women workers. The courts interpreted similar legislation for men as an infringement of the freedom of contract but allowed it for women because of their supposed weakness and need for special protection. An equal rights amendment (ERA) would likely have knocked down those hard-fought gains. ERA supporters such as Alice Paul (who wrote its original language in 1923) argued that these laws restricted women's economic rights, were demeaning in their stereotyped views of women, and hindered, rather than helped women on the job. So divisive was this issue that it basically split the feminist movement into two camps until the 1960s, by which time the extension of workplace protection to both sexes had made protective legislation for women unnecessary.

Despite the booming economy of the 1920s (in 1927 the Ford Motor Company produced an automobile every twenty-four seconds), the prosperity was not equally distributed: the top 5 percent of the nation's households received one-third of the national income. The onset of the Great Depression in 1929 exposed the economy's underlying structural weaknesses. It also showed how gender—as well as class, race, and geography—affected the experience of hard times.

In many ways men and women experienced the Depression differently, both in families and on the job. When a man lost his job, he lost his role as breadwinner for his family, but none of the nation's housewives lost their jobs. On the contrary, contributions to their families took on new significance with husbands out of work. By substituting their own labor for goods and services previously purchased, housewives could stretch the family budget to cover periods of unemployment or cuts in pay. Robert and Helen Lynd described this phenomenon in *Middletown in Transition* (1937), their sociological study of Muncie, Indiana: "The men, cut adrift from their usual routine, lost much of their sense of time and dawdled helplessly and dully about the streets; while in the homes the women's world remained largely intact and the round of cooking, housecleaning, and mending became if anything more absorbing." Few were comfortable with this deviation from traditional gender roles. "We had no choice," one woman recalled. "We just did what had to be done one day at a time." These were the women Eleanor Roosevelt addressed in *It's Up to the Women*.

Women also helped their families by taking jobs: the number of married women working doubled during the decade. It probably seems counterintuitive that women could find jobs when one-quarter of the workforce was unemployed, but the answer is linked to the gendered occupational structure of the economy. Male workers were concentrated in the very sectors hardest hit by the economic collapse: manufacturing, heavy industry, coal mining, and construction. Women's jobs in the clerical and retail fields or domestic and personal service were somewhat less affected by the downturn, although they still faced accusations that they were taking jobs away from men. Addressing that charge, one commentator noted astutely, "Few of the people who oppose married women's employment seem to realize that a coal miner or a steel worker cannot very well fit the jobs of nursemaids, cleaning women, or the factory and clerical jobs now filled by women." Such stereotyping afforded women a small measure of protection in the economic crisis, but at the cost of confirming their concentration in lower-status, low-paying jobs.

The Depression affected racial minorities harshly. Mexican Americans in the Southwest and West who had found a toehold in agricultural and industrial work in the 1920s—one-quarter of Mexican and Mexican American female workers were employed in the garment industry or in canneries in 1930—faced extreme discrimination once hard times hit. One response was forced repatriation to Mexico: from 1931 to 1934 one-third of the Mexican American population (some five hundred thousand people) returned to Mexico either voluntarily or under threat of deportation, further disrupting families already hurting because of the Depression. Mexican American women founded mutual aid societies (*mutualistas*) in their communities to counter the racism and economic hardship they experienced in the broader society.

For other groups, such as African Americans, the hard times of the 1930s were not all that different from normal times. As poet Langston Hughes observed, "The depression brought everybody down a peg or two. And Negroes had few pegs to fall." The Great Migration out of the South that had surged in the 1910s and 1920s (bringing 1.3 million migrants to the North and West) slowed dramatically in the 1930s, when jobs dried up in urban areas. Even domestic work, the mainstay for black women, was often undercut by white women now willing to take those jobs to earn a meager wage.

The New Deal responded to this broad economic crisis with a mix of relief programs, stimulus spending, and economic reforms. Much later than western European countries, the United States in the 1930s implemented the rudiments of a modern welfare state—that is, the federal government accepted responsibility for the successful performance of the economy and guaranteeing the basic needs of its citizens. Government relief made a real difference to communities that federal programs had never before reached, such as the Mexican American community in El Paso and San Francisco's Chinatown. And women played a large role in this process.

8. Dorothea Lange took this photograph of a woman and her two children at a "pea-pickers" camp in Nipomo, California, in 1936 to document migratory farm labor conditions for the Farm Security Administration.

Following Eleanor Roosevelt's stellar example, women took on new roles in politics and government in the 1930s. The dramatic expansion of New Deal social welfare programs provided jobs and opportunities for professional women long active in those fields;

women's expertise was especially crucial to the Works Progress Administration and the Social Security Administration. Women also took on larger roles in the revitalized Democratic Party. Bound together in an informal network, women such as Frances Perkins, Ellen Sullivan Woodward, and Molly Dewson showed not just the continuity between Progressive era reform and the New Deal but also demonstrated women's new postsuffrage roles.

Ordinary women fared less well in New Deal programs, which were often organized around the principle of male breadwinners and their dependent wives. Not every woman had a man to head her household, so they had to fight with relief workers for recognition of their plight. Custom also limited their options: the Works Progress Administration put millions of men to work on construction and industrial jobs but confined women's relief work to sewing rooms, schools, and playgrounds. One-quarter of the labor codes established to jumpstart the economy allowed women workers to be paid less than men; agricultural and domestic work, where women predominated, were initially excluded from Social Security and the Fair Labor Standards Act coverage. And popular programs like the Civilian Conservation Corps were limited to men only, leading critics to ask, "Where is the she-she-she?" Without the effective mobilization of the women's network, women's needs for relief might have been overlooked, if not forgotten completely, but the results were far from equitable. Still, even these token efforts often meant the difference between making do and doing without.

Another area of dramatic growth for women in the 1930s was in the labor movement. Once the federal government put its force behind labor's right to organize with the Wagner Labor Relations Act of 1935, women's union participation surged, from 250,000 in 1929 to more than 800,000 by the end of the 1930s. Union membership meant higher wages, better benefits, and job security for women as well as men. And these new union members were not just white ethnic industrial workers: unionized garment workers in Chinatown waged a successful strike against the National Dollar Stores in 1938, and Mexican American women in the cannery industry in California created the powerful United Cannery, Agricultural, Packing and Allied Workers of America in 1937.

Despite all the programs streaming out of Washington, the New Deal never solved the problem of the Depression: spending for World War II did. Indeed the cloud of ominous developments abroad hangs over the 1930s, especially the rise of Nazi Germany and the aggressive expansion of Japan in the Pacific. Strongly isolationist sentiment limited Franklin Roosevelt's ability to commit the United States to the global war, which began in Europe in 1939, but the economy was already moving toward a war footing before the decisive Japanese attack on Pearl Harbor on December 7, 1941. America was now at war, and American women were, too.

Probably the best known wartime image of a woman is Rosie the Riveter, from Norman Rockwell's iconic *Saturday Evening Post* cover portraying a muscular defense worker in coveralls cradling her riveting gun while she eats her lunch. The dramatic increase in defense production quickly absorbed all the leftover unemployment from the 1930s and necessitated the recruitment of a new workforce—the nation's women—now that the nation's men were off at war. But Rosie was not just a patriotic housewife who took a job "for the duration": many women already in the labor force used wartime labor shortages to move up into better paying industrial jobs. They also moved geographically, often leaving home for the first time; California, the site of major defense mobilization, gained 1.4 million newcomers. This wartime climate was especially liberating for single women, who seized opportunities for increased autonomy and independence in their work and personal lives. Things were not quite as easy for African American, Mexican American, and Chinese American women, but they, too, found opportunities because of the wartime emergency. In all, the female workforce grew 50 percent between 1940 and 1945.

Some 350,000 women played an even more direct role in the war effort by joining the 15 million men who served in the military. The largest number—some 140,000—served with the Women's Army Corps (WAC), followed by 100,000 in the WAVES (Women Appointed for Volunteer Emergency Service) of the navy. A special group of women pilots made up the Women Airforce Service Pilots (WASP). Tasked with ferrying planes between various domestic airbases, these spunky women loved the chance to combine their passion for flying with service to their country, even though it cost thirty-eight lives. Their experiences reflected the combination of opportunity and sexism that was the lot of women in the military: they were restricted to the continental United States and denied opportunities for promotion, and their program was phased out as soon as male pilots started returning from service abroad. Like Rosie the Riveter, new roles were acceptable only if they were temporary.

Japanese American women had no choice about their wartime roles: along with the men and children in their West Coast communities, they were forcibly detained in internment camps in the aftermath of Pearl Harbor. "Shikata ga nai" (It can't be helped) was their stoical response. Conditions in the euphemistically named "relocation centers" located in remote sections of California, Nevada, and other western states, were especially difficult for women trying to keep up some semblance of family normalcy but were also hard for husbands, who lost their roles as heads of household in these communal settings. The policy began to ease in 1943 and 1944, in part because of a shortage of agricultural labor, but the wartime internment of 110,000 Japanese Americans remains a giant blot on the history of civil liberties in the United States.

IT'S A WOMAN'S WAR TOO!

JOIN THE
WAVES
YOUR COUNTRY NEEDS YOU NOW

JOHN FALTER USNR

Apply to your nearest
NAVY RECRUITING STATION OR OFFICE OF NAVAL OFFICER PROCUREMENT

9. With the slogan "It's a woman's war too!" this 1942 recruiting poster encouraged women to join the WAVES, the women's unit of the U.S. Navy.

Japanese relocation

Monica (Itoi) Sone's autobiography, *Nisei Daughter* (1953), tells the story of Japanese relocation through the perspective of a young woman. Here she describes her family's evacuation to a temporary encampment; later "Family #10710" will be sent to a permanent camp in Idaho.

All through the night I heard people getting up, dragging cots around. I stared at our little window, unable to sleep. I was glad Mother had put up a makeshift curtain on the window for I noticed a powerful beam of light sweeping across it every few seconds. The lights came from high towers placed around the camp where guards with Tommy guns kept a twenty-four hour vigil. I remembered the wire fence encircling us, and a knot of anger tightened in my breast. What was I doing behind a fence like a criminal? If there were accusations to be made, why hadn't I been given a fair trial? Maybe I wasn't considered an American anymore....

Of one thing I was sure. The wire fence was real. I no longer had the right to walk out of it. It was because I had Japanese ancestors. It was also because some people had little faith in the ideas and ideals of democracy. They said that after all these were but words and could not possibly insure loyalty. New laws and camps were surer devices. I finally buried my face in my pillow to wipe out burning thoughts and snatch what sleep I could.

The war had a different impact on the Chinese American community, which benefited from the wartime alliance between China and the United States. As a gesture toward better relations, the 1943 repeal of the Chinese Exclusion Act of 1882 allowed some forty thousand Chinese women to enter the country over the next two decades. War brides married to American soldiers, including many from China, the Philippines, Australia, and Europe, were also allowed to take up legal residence in the United States.

War's end brought the soldiers home but did not lead to a stable international situation. Deteriorating relations with the Soviet Union set in motion the Cold War, which gripped the country through the 1960s. Fear of communism poisoned domestic politics, leading to loyalty oaths, witch hunts for subversives in government, and other forms of repression subsumed under the rubric "McCarthyism," named for the Wisconsin senator who was its most forceful champion. Because many politically active women had been involved in now suspect left-wing causes in the 1930s and 1940s, they found themselves under increased scrutiny. Some lost jobs or security clearances; others learned to hide their political pasts. Betty Friedan, for example, totally erased her stint as a left-wing labor journalist in the late 1940s when she presented herself as an ordinary and apolitical suburban housewife in her 1963 best seller *The Feminine Mystique*.

And what about the Rosie the Riveters? They, too, lost their jobs, to returning veterans. Women understood that—they were grateful to the men who had served—but it was harder to stomach when experienced women were passed over for nonveteran men when new hiring started up. Instead of trading their overalls for aprons at home, many defense workers simply went back to the traditional jobs available to women. The percentage of women in the workforce dropped slightly after the war but by 1950 was back up to 28.6 percent. While historians debate whether World War II was a major turning point for American women, it definitely encouraged the trend of women working that had been steadily building since the nineteenth century.

The struggle for equality and diversity

In the 1950s television challenged movies as the dominant form of American popular culture and supplied some of the most enduring images of the decade as a time of suburban, family-oriented bliss. Just saying the names of the shows—*Leave It to Beaver, Ozzie and Harriet, Father Knows Best,* and *I Love*

Lucy, among others—conjures up visions of backyard play sets and white picket fences, with Chevy station wagons parked in the driveways. And yet scratch the surface of American life, especially for its women, and the picture is far more complicated.

Like the 1920s, the decade of the 1950s is recalled as an age of affluence. Despite fears of a return to depression conditions when World War II ended, the economy entered a period of extended growth that brought increased wealth and social and economic mobility to a wider swath of the American population. With jobs plentiful and wages good, couples could marry earlier: by 1951, a third of all American women were married by age nineteen. In a total aberration from long-term trends, the birthrate shot up in what demographers call the "baby boom," peaking in 1957. Now the average woman was having close to four children. Selling consumer goods and services to these growing families fueled the economy and prompted a major expansion of the nation's educational system.

Betty Friedan later skewered this suburban lifestyle in *The Feminine Mystique*, especially its insistence that "the highest value and the only commitment for women is the fulfillment of their own femininity." While some women, mainly white and middle-class, felt trapped in the suburbs, Friedan's stark picture of "the problem that has no name" was misleading. For example, many families still could not afford to live the child-centered suburban existence so lavishly profiled in women's magazines like *McCall's* and *Good Housekeeping*. What relevance did stay-at-home domesticity have for black or Latina women trapped in poor urban neighborhoods, farm women struggling in rural areas, or working-class families still striving for a toehold in American society? Finally, singling out young white mothers with small children as representative of the 1950s skews the picture. We think of these women as forever frozen in time, yet this was only a short stage in their lives. Even with four children, these wives would be done with their intensive childrearing responsibilities by their late thirties, leaving them with at least three or four more decades of their adult lives to fill.

By far the biggest challenge to the domesticated view of the 1950s is the number of women who continued to stream into the workforce, including married women with children who should have been the prime candidates for the heightened emphasis on domesticity. By 1960 more than one-third of women held jobs outside the home. And most of these women worked for economic reasons: supporting the new consumer-oriented lifestyles of televisions, automobiles, and family vacations often took two incomes instead of just one, even in a time of affluence. (This trend accelerated as the economy stagnated later in the twentieth century.) And unlike the Depression, women were often welcomed into the workforce, where their preponderance in fields like clerical work, teaching, and health care provision dovetailed well with the needs of the postindustrial economy.

Challenging the perception of the 1950s as an era of conformity and political apathy, women were major agents of change in the postwar period. Groups like the League of Women Voters continued to provide an entry point for women into local civic activities. The political parties welcomed, indeed would have been lost without, the female grassroots volunteer. Women in the labor movement worked to consolidate the gains of the 1930s and 1940s, and progressive women came together in groups, such as Women Strike for Peace, to support disarmament and the banning of nuclear testing.

Black women played especially large roles in the emerging civil rights movement, which had roots at least as far back as the 1930s and escalated during World War II, what is called "the long civil rights movement." The 1954 Supreme Court decision in *Brown v. Board of Education*, which outlawed segregation in schools, was an early legal victory. Then the focus shifted to public confrontations: the 1955–1956 bus boycott in Montgomery,

Alabama, after Rosa Parks was arrested for not giving up her seat on a local bus; the tense situation in 1957 when six teenaged girls and three boys integrated Little Rock High School; the sit-ins that targeted segregated public accommodations such as lunch counters in 1960 and 1961; and the Freedom Rides that simultaneously challenged segregation on interstate bus travel. Black women were central to all these actions. Ella Baker, one of these trailblazing women, said it best: "The movement of the fifties and sixties was carried largely by women."

Yet the dominant images of the Civil Rights movement mainly revolve around black men, often ministers, led by Reverend Martin Luther King Jr. Tellingly, all the original speakers for the much-lauded March on Washington in 1963 were men. And yet to focus just on the publicly recognized national leaders misses the energy and support at the grassroots level supplied by black women. Grounded in the daily struggle for survival, black women knew who to turn to and how to get things done in their communities. Recruiting friends and relatives through existing kin and friendship networks, women quickly found themselves on the front lines of boycotts, voter registration drives, demonstrations, even acts of civil disobedience that landed them in jail.

Civil rights pioneers risked their careers and even their lives for the cause. Ella Baker, who served as a mentor to the rising generation of student activists, was an impassioned believer in participatory democracy whose motto was "strong people don't need strong leaders." Rosa Parks was not just a tired seamstress but a longtime activist in her local National Association for the Advancement of Colored People. Fannie Lou Hamer became a field secretary for the Student Non-Violent Coordinating Committee after being denied the right to register to vote in Mississippi. Daisy Bates provided physical and emotional support to the "Little Rock Nine" during the desegregation struggle. Representing the younger generation, Ruby Doris Smith was severely beaten while participating in the Freedom Rides, and Diane Nash led sit-ins in Nashville while a student at Fisk University; both later were active in the Student Non-Violent Coordinating Committee.

As the civil rights movement gathered steam in the early 1960s, another movement—that of women—was on the horizon. While there had not been a mass women's movement since the final days of suffrage, feminism was far from dead in the postsuffrage era. Rather, women carried on the struggle individually in a range of venues: politics, labor unions, on the job, in the professions, in creative fields. In effect they kept the suffrage momentum going until it was time for another mass mobilization to coalesce. This revival of feminism (often called "second wave feminism" to distinguish it from the first wave of suffrage) had its roots in the 1960s and found its fullest flowering in the first half of the 1970s.

At the risk of oversimplifying a complex phenomenon, two different strands of feminism fueled this revival. The first was women's rights activism. Many women's rights advocates served in appointive or elective office at various levels of government, and they knew each other through overlapping professional networks. An important spur was the creation of the President's Commission on the Status of Women in 1961 under the leadership of Eleanor Roosevelt. The commission's final report, issued in 1963, was a fairly tame call for more equity in the workplace and family life, but it did encourage the passage of the Equal Pay Act of 1963. The addition of "sex" to Title VII of the Civil Rights Act of 1964 was an even more far-reaching legislative achievement because it gave women a crucial legal tool with which to challenge workplace discrimination. In turn the enthusiastic reaction to Betty Friedan's *Feminine Mystique* suggested a groundswell of popular dissatisfaction with contemporary women's lives. In 1966 a group of women led by Friedan formed the National Organization for Women, which styled itself as a civil rights organization for women. Soon it was the largest feminist organization in the country.

Women's liberation represented the second strand of feminism. In contrast to their more mainstream women's rights counterparts, women's liberationists were younger and more radical. They came to feminism through participation in civil rights and the anti–Vietnam War movement, which had increased their confidence but also fed frustration when they were primarily treated as coffee makers, note takers, and sex objects. ("Girls say yes to boys who say no.") By 1967 and 1968 radical women realized they needed a movement of their own. Eschewing traditional membership and leadership structures, women's liberation was all mass, no organization.

One of the most distinctive features of this brand of feminism was its embrace of the maxim "the personal is political." Women came together in consciousness-raising sessions to talk honestly and often painfully about their lives. As radical feminist Shulamith Firestone said, "Three months of this sort of thing is enough to make a feminist of any woman." Operating independently in major cities, women's liberation went public at the 1968 Miss America Pageant, where protestors crowned a live sheep and deposited items of female oppression such as girdles and bras in a freedom trash can. Contrary to urban myth, no bras were burned, but the reputation of feminists as bra burners stuck.

After developing separately, the two strands began to coalesce around 1970. By now the media had discovered feminism. Coverage of events like the Women's Strike for Equality, commemorating the fiftieth anniversary of suffrage on August 26, 1970, brought the ideas of this powerful new movement to a much wider audience. Although still an object of derision and jest, the women's movement (as it was now referred to) managed quite a few accomplishments in a short period of time. In 1972 Congress passed the Equal Rights Amendment, and Shirley Chisholm, an African American member of Congress from New York, ran for president. Congress passed Title IX of the Education Amendments Act of 1972, which prohibited sex discrimination in all aspects of education and provided a huge spur to women's sports. In January 1973 the Supreme Court upheld women's constitutional right to abortion in the far-reaching *Roe v. Wade* decision. Later that year feminist tennis star Billie Jean King trounced Bobby Riggs in the nationally televised Battle of the Sexes. Suddenly the topic of women, which had been a dead issue just a decade before, was squarely on the national agenda.

Black and Chicana feminism also surged, and not just as a reaction to feeling unwelcome in the predominantly white women's movement, although that certainly was a factor. These women took their own separate roads to feminism. Black feminism had its roots in changes in the civil rights movement, specifically the embrace of black power, which prioritized the experiences of black men. More broadly, black feminism affirmed that attention had to be paid to race and class as well as to gender in order to understand the complexity of black women's lives. The Combahee River Collective, a group of black feminists in the Boston/Cambridge area, penned one of the most influential pieces of black feminist theory in 1977. Looking at "what oppression is comprised of on a day-to-day basis," they refused to separate the multiple oppressions that shaped black women's lives, including homophobia.

Chicana feminism also emerged independently from white feminism, starting around 1969 and 1970 as an effort to increase the visibility and influence of women within the broader Chicano movement. Chicana feminists proudly pointed to a tradition of activism on the part of their Mexican foremothers, as well as the large roles women played in Mexican American civil rights groups in the 1940s and 1950s. In addition, labor activists such as Dolores Huerta and Jessie Lopez De La Cruz took key leadership roles in the United Farm Workers of America, which began organizing in the fields of the San Joaquin valley in 1962. The first National Chicana Conference was held in Houston in 1971.

Chicana labor activism

When Jessie De La Cruz joined forces with labor activist Cesar Chavez in what participants called La Causa, she was forty-two years old, married, and the mother of six children and had been a farmworker her entire life. She later became a paid union official.

> I think I was made an organizer because in the first place I could relate to the farmworkers, being a lifelong farmworker. I was well-known in the small towns around Fresno. Wherever I went to speak to them, they listened. I told them about how we were excluded from the NLRB in 1935, how we had no benefits, no minimum wage, nothing out in the fields—no restrooms, nothing. I would talk about how we were paid what the grower wanted to pay us, and how we couldn't set a price on our work. I explained that we could do something about these things by joining a union, by working together....
>
> It was hard being a woman organizer. Many of our people my age and older were raised with the old customs in Mexico: where the husband rules, he is king of his house. The wife obeys, and the children, too. So when we first started it was very, very hard....
>
> It doesn't take courage. All it takes is standing up for what you believe in, talking about things that you know are true, things that should be happening, instead of what is happening. That's all it takes.

White, black, and Chicana feminism are all examples of identity politics—that is, the creation of a self-identified social group, usually in opposition to the dominant society. Identity politics was also extremely important to the emergence of gay liberation, commonly dated to the 1969 Stonewall Riot in New York City, when patrons at a gay bar fought back against police harassment. In order to demand better treatment and recognition as a group, men and women first had to articulate and accept their shared identity as gay.

Feminism made particular sense to lesbians, who found the movement a supportive atmosphere in which to explore their connections with other women. Some heterosexual feminists at first saw the issue of lesbianism as a tangent or, worse yet, a liability, in their quest for broader public acceptance; Friedan, for example, publicly complained of a "lavender menace." And yet the realization that lesbians faced many of the same problems as other women eventually caused the gay/straight split to ease. Exemplified by towering poets and writers such as Audre Lorde, Adrienne Rich, and Gloria Anzaldúa, a lesbian feminist perspective has been especially important in the fields of literature, poetry, and criticism, as well as women's studies.

Feminists found all this change exhilarating: they really thought they were going to change the world. But powerful social movements run the risk of provoking equally powerful backlashes, which began to happen in the mid-1970s as women, and more than a few men, grew concerned about the rapidity of social change and openly challenged feminist goals. The Equal Rights Amendment and abortion became the main flashpoints.

When the Equal Rights Amendment passed Congress in 1972, activists expected speedy ratification; by 1974, thirty-four states (out of a necessary thirty-eight) had ratified the amendment. But then the momentum stopped dead in its tracks, except for Indiana in 1977. Activists won a three-year extension on the ratification deadline until 1982, but extensive lobbying in Florida, North Carolina, and Illinois failed to convince legislators to pass the amendment, and it went down to defeat.

A prime reason for this defeat was conservative Republican activist Phyllis Schlafly, whose organization STOP ERA first targeted the issue in 1972 and then mobilized masses of grassroots women, especially from evangelical churches and right-wing groups, against ratification. The ranks of ERA opponents were swelled by those who feared that women had more to lose than

10. Women picket the White House in 1977, rallying opposition to the Equal Rights Amendment, which they feared would cause women to be drafted and lose social security benefits.

gain by the sweeping (and false) changes attributed to it, such as undermining the husband's responsibility to provide for his family, abolishing child support and alimony, and forcing women into the workforce, to say nothing of unisex toilets. Opponents, often wearing aprons and bringing home-baked apple pies to legislators as part of their anti-ERA lobbying, self-consciously demonstrated their commitment to traditional gender roles. Women have supplied a key constituency, especially at the grassroots level, for conservative initiatives ever since.

Conflicts over who spoke for American women were on full display at the 1977 National Women's Conference in Houston, convened in connection with the United Nations International Decade of Women. Some twenty thousand delegates came together to pass a national plan of action that included support for abortion, lesbian rights, and the ERA. Across town, in a counter-conference organized by Schlafly and her supporters, almost as many women loudly asserted their allegiance to more

Conservative complaints about Title IX

Phyllis Schlafly took issue with the Education Amendments of 1972, popularly known as Title IX, in her newsletter, the *Phyllis Schlafly Report*. Here she criticizes the regulations drafted by the Department of Health, Education and Welfare to carry out the law.

The HEW Regulation is based on the "gender-free" approach demanded by the women's lib militants. It is dogma of the women's lib radicals that there really is no difference between men and women (except the sex organs), and they demand that everything touched by Federal and state law, bureaucratic regulation, the educational system, and public funding be absolutely "gender-free" so that males and females have identical treatment....

We reject the "gender-free" approach. We believe that there are many differences between male and female, and that we are entitled to have our laws, regulations, schools, and courts reflect these differences and allow for reasonable differences in treatment that reasonable men and women want.

We reject the argument that sex discrimination should be treated the same as race discrimination. There is vastly more difference between a man and a woman than there is between a black and a white, and it is nonsense to adopt a legal and bureaucratic attitude that pretends that those differences do not exist....

In summary, we believe that the HEW Regulation on prohibiting sex discrimination is offensive to the big majority of American women and men. It reflects the narrow view of women's lib militants who are determined to force their goals on our educational institutions whether the rest of us like them or not.

traditional gender roles, especially the fundamental differences between the sexes, which they saw as the basis for family and civic life. These internal conflicts, plus a swing to the right in the political climate, completed by Ronald Reagan's election in 1980, ushered in a period of stalemate and retrenchment for the women's movement.

In hindsight, however, abortion, not the ERA, proved most divisive. When the Supreme Court handed down its decision in *Roe v. Wade* in 1973, it stepped into a minefield of controversy. Feminists acclaimed women's newly legal constitutional right to abortion, but opponents immediately mobilized to overturn the decision. An increasingly powerful "right to life" movement placed the rights of the fetus ahead of the right of the woman to decide whether to carry a pregnancy to term. In 1977 Congress passed the Hyde Amendment, which prohibited federal funds from paying for abortions for welfare recipients even if the procedure was necessary to save the life of the mother; in 1980 the Supreme Court upheld the law.

Finding insufficient support for a constitutional amendment stating that human life starts at conception, and perhaps mindful of the recent ratification difficulties of the ERA, antiabortion activists chose another strategy: systematically chipping away at the provision of abortion services. Following the logic of *Roe v. Wade*, which affirmed women's constitutional right to abortion in the first trimester of pregnancy but opened the door to state regulation after that point, abortion opponents pushed state and federal legislation requiring, among other limits or restrictions, parental or spousal consent, mandated waiting periods, and the outlawing of certain late-term procedures; all of these restrictions were upheld by the Supreme Court. At the same time violence and intimidation against abortion providers caused many clinics to close, leaving women in large swaths of the country without easy access to a legal abortion.

The country remains deeply divided between prochoice and prolife stances, with support strongest for access to abortion in the first trimester (twelve weeks) and in the case of rape, incest, or the life of the mother being threatened. These ongoing debates, which really are as much about women's rights as about abortion, show that many of the changes associated with second wave feminism are still being contested decades later.

Continuity and change in American women's lives

In 1965 Congress legislated a significant change in immigration policy, abandoning the quota system from the 1920s that had discriminated against Asians and southern and eastern Europeans and expanding the ability of relatives to join family members already legally resident in the country. Many immigrants from Mexico, as well as Central and South America and the Caribbean, took advantage of this second option. The law also opened the doors to Vietnamese and Cambodian refugees who were fleeing turmoil and instability after the American withdrawal from Southeast Asia. What was so profoundly different about this round of post-1965 immigration was that women came in equal numbers to men, or greater, and that newly arrived immigrant women, including wives, joined the labor force in numbers comparable to native-born American women.

New arrivals usually entered the economic structure at the very bottom, taking the least desirable jobs such as domestic service. And when they exited domestic service, they often were relegated to "dirty work" such as cleaning rooms in hotels and offices or changing bedpans in hospitals and nursing homes. The willingness of recent immigrants to take such jobs happened in tandem with an expansion of options for African American women. As a result, the percentage of black women who were domestic servants fell from almost 40 percent in 1960 to just 2 percent in 1990.

Recent immigrants, indeed all Americans, faced a more challenging economic climate as the twentieth century concluded. As the country moved into a postindustrial, service-oriented economy, many relatively well paid industrial jobs disappeared, often outsourced to other countries, such as China, and the gap between rich and poor widened, especially after the 1980s. The economic pressures on women to work intensified to the point where most women, even those with small children, now expected to work for most of their lives. Unfortunately, the lack of affordable day care made it difficult to combine work and family roles. In contrast to the benefits offered to working mothers in western European democracies, American women were just expected to cope on their own.

Despite the opening of many industrial and professional jobs to women, almost three-quarters of the female labor force remained in predominantly female occupations, such as teaching, nursing, clerical and sales work, and personal service. And along with women's work went women's wages, although the gap shrank somewhat. By 2002 the median wage for full-time women workers, which had been 59 percent of men's in 1970, had risen to 77 percent. While the gap between the wages of white and black women had also shrunk, the wages of Latinas and recent immigrants continued to lag behind.

American families were also changing. Despite nostalgia for the model of male breadwinner and female housewife, at the end of the twentieth century this pattern applied only to a tiny minority of families. In most two-parent households both adults worked, sometimes at multiple jobs. The biggest change was the number of women living outside traditional marriage. In this category were the large number of single mothers, mainly divorced, separated, or widowed women raising children, joined by a much smaller number of single women who chose to have children on their own. By 2000 approximately one out of three children was born to an unmarried mother. Given women's generally lower wages, these female-headed households often hovered near the poverty line in what sociologists call the feminization of poverty.

Same-sex partners also headed a growing number of families, their rights, including the right to marry, increasingly recognized by legislatures, the courts, and public opinion. The new visibility for gay men and lesbians, indeed the widening of options for sexual expression encapsulated in the acronym LGBTQ (lesbian, gay, bisexual, transgender, and queer and/or questioning), took place in a media culture that increasingly blurred the lines between public and private. A prime example was the much-publicized coming out of comedian Ellen DeGeneres both on her television show and in real life in 1997. That public/private line became even more porous as social networking facilitated the sharing of a vast amount of personal data online.

Popular culture and the media could be both liberating and oppressive for women. Many aspects of popular culture challenged traditional gender roles, encouraged the embrace of new behaviors, and provided a soundtrack of music and film as a guide to personal as well as political liberation. But other aspects of popular culture were less emancipatory, especially images that promoted an often unattainable ideal of female beauty and appearance. No wonder women have a love-hate relationship with the media.

At times the media circulated misleading and deceptive information about women. A telling example: the 1986 cover story in *Newsweek* that claimed single women in their forties had a greater chance of being killed by a terrorist attack than marrying. The statistic was wrong, but the media used it to imply that feminism's new freedoms had been bad for women and that it was time to retreat. Journalist Susan Faludi offered a counter-argument: it was not feminism's fault that women were struggling with the challenges of their new lives; it was that the feminist revolution had not gone far enough to restructure those lives.

These debates played out especially at the level of elite women and their options. The media remained fascinated by women's struggle to "have it all"—marriage, career, and children—especially if women opted out of high-powered, high-paying jobs to return to the status of full-time homemaker. Note that only a tiny proportion of women were in the top echelons of corporate or professional life to begin with, and an even tinier number made this choice. Most working women could not afford to stay home with their kids even if they wanted to.

This ongoing debate shows that while there have been revolutionary changes in certain aspects of women's lives, notably the expectation of waged labor, in other areas the changes have been less dramatic, generally just leaving individual women to muddle through on their own. Perhaps one of the most positive recent shifts is that balancing work and family is increasingly seen not just as a women's issue but also relevant to men. But at the end of day, despite men's shouldering a larger share of domestic work and child care, it is still primarily the working woman who adds a second shift at home when her regular job is done.

Working women continue to face sexual harassment on the job, but now they have legal recourse to challenge what used to be accepted as "the way things were"—men's inappropriate behavior toward female coworkers, including sexual insults, lewd or inappropriate comments, and fondling or pinching. In the 1980s feminist legal scholar Catherine MacKinnon pioneered the argument that sexual harassment, defined as a hostile workplace for women, was covered by the prohibitions against sex discrimination contained in Title VII of the Civil Rights Act of 1964. In the case of *Meritor Savings Bank v. Vinson* (1986) the Supreme Court accepted that reasoning.

Sexual harassment took center stage in the confirmation hearings of Clarence Thomas for appointment to the U.S. Supreme Court in 1991. Several women who had worked with Thomas at the

Department of Education and the Economic Employment Opportunity Commission informally contacted the Senate Judiciary Committee with allegations of sexual harassment, but only at the end of the hearings was one of the accusers, law professor Anita Hill, allowed to testify. Providing compelling details about patterns of inappropriate sexual conversations and behavior on the part of her former boss, Anita Hill's testimony failed to sway the all-male committee, which narrowly recommended Thomas's nomination. The fact that both Hill and Thomas were African American introduced a complicated interplay of race and gender, but many women instantly understood what Hill had endured. Building on the public perception that male politicians just "didn't get it," a surge of female candidates in the 1992 election brought the total in the Senate to six.

The broader story of women in politics and public life showed dramatic progress coupled with lingering barriers. California congresswoman Nancy Pelosi rose to a major leadership position in the House of Representatives, and Madeleine K. Albright, Condoleezza Rice, and Hillary Rodham Clinton all served as secretary of state. The Supreme Court boasted three female justices: Ruth Bader Ginsburg, Sonia Sotomayor, and Elena Kagan. Women of both major parties served as governors, and former Alaska governor Sarah Palin ran for vice president on the 2008 Republican ticket. But even with recent electoral gains that increased the number of women senators to twenty in 2012, parity is still a long way in the future.

This shifting balance sheet between how much progress has occurred versus how much remains to be done can also be seen in the area of pay equity. The case of Lilly Ledbetter is fairly typical of the problems women face in the modern workplace but atypical in its ultimate outcome. Ledbetter had worked as a supervisor in a Goodyear Tire assembly plant in Alabama since 1979, the kind of well-paid job that previously would have been reserved for men;

only as she approached retirement did she learn that she had been paid significantly less than men with the same seniority and job descriptions. She sued Goodyear and won back pay and damages, but the case was overturned by the Supreme Court in 2007 because of an Economic Employment Opportunity Commission rule that such claims must be filed within 180 days of when the discrimination first occurred—which in her case was back in 1979. In the end, the story had a happy ending: new federal legislation that restarted the 180-day clock every time a discriminatory paycheck was issued. The Lilly Ledbetter Fair Pay Act of 2009 was the first piece of legislation signed by President Barack Obama.

Many of these workplace challenges affect women in the military, probably the area of modern life still most associated with men and masculinity. Like the modern economy, the modern military found it could not function without the skills performed by women in civilian life, especially clerical work and nursing. The issue of women in the military got caught up in the debate over the ERA in the 1970s, when opponents questioned whether the amendment would require women to be drafted alongside men. The amendment's supporters tried to dodge the issue by saying either that no one should be drafted (this was at the tail end of the Vietnam War) or that the draft was a matter to be legislated by Congress. Indeed, when President Jimmy Carter proposed reinstating the draft in 1980, women were specifically excluded, a policy that was upheld by the Supreme Court in *Rostker v. Goldberg* (1981).

But feminism was having an impact even on the military. In 1976 the military academies opened to women, with the first classes graduating from West Point and Annapolis in 1980. As the United States moved to an all-volunteer army after Vietnam, it increasingly depended on women volunteers, who were generally better educated and easier to recruit than men. Many women, especially those from racial minorities or working-class backgrounds, found the military an attractive career path, even though they were still barred from many specialties and from serving in combat, exemptions that effectively limited their upward mobility. In 1991 more than forty thousand women were deployed to Iraq in Operation Desert Shield and Operation Desert Storm, and thirteen women lost their lives. How quickly attitudes had changed: in the 1970s the idea of drafting women, let alone the prospect that they might be killed in service to their country alongside men, was unthinkable. Still, it took until 2012 before the ban on women in combat was fully lifted.

Unfortunately, women in the armed forces fought many of their battles not against enemy combatants but against the aggressively male culture of the military itself. A staggering one out of three service women reported being victims of sexual assault, including rape, during their enlistments. If they tried to press charges, they often found male superiors more concerned with preserving the career prospects of the male perpetrators than with giving justice to the victimized women. Lesbians in the military faced additional challenges: under the "don't ask/don't tell" policy instituted in 1994, they risked severance from service if their sexual orientation became known. After that policy was revoked in 2011, lesbians with children struggled with the disruption of deployment, the lack of support services for gay families, and lingering homophobia. And yet women, who made up 14.5 percent of the armed forces in 2011, continued to see military life as a desirable option. New opportunities coupled with ongoing challenges: what better summation of the lives of modern American women at the end of the twentieth century?

Another end point—the Fourth International Women's Conference, held in Beijing in 1995—harks back to the internationalism of the nineteenth-century abolitionist and woman suffrage movements while also recognizing the increasing globalization of American life. The United Nations convened the First International Women's Conference in Mexico City in 1975, kicking off the UN Decade of Women, and it was followed by conferences in Copenhagen in 1980 and Nairobi in 1985. At each gathering, American women came together with women from throughout the world to talk about common problems and challenges. The Beijing conference was especially noteworthy for its articulation of the idea that women's rights are human rights, as First Lady Hillary Rodham Clinton forcefully argued in a keynote address. American women no longer needed to stop their activism at the border or limit it to one gender. They were now part of a truly global community.

References

Introduction

Gerda Lerner, *Teaching Women's History* (Washington, D.C.: American Historical Association, 1981), 16.

Linda Gordon, *U.S. Women's History* (Washington, D.C.: American Historical Association, 1997), 2.

Mary R. Beard, *Woman as Force in History* (New York: Macmillan, 1946).

"Gerda Lerner on the Future of Our Past," interview by Catharine R. Stimpson, *Ms.* 10 (September 1981), 94, 96.

Chapter 1

"Bow or a sifter?" quoted in *Sifters: Native American Women's Lives*, ed. Theda Perdue (New York: Oxford University Press, 2001), 3.

"Laws of Virginia: 1662," in *The Statutes at Large, Being a Collection of All the Laws of Virginia*, ed. William Waller Hening (Charlottesville: University Press of Virginia, 1969), 2:270.

Anne Bradstreet, "To My Dear and Loving Husband," in *The Works of Anne Bradstreet*, ed. Jeannine Hensley (Cambridge, Mass.: Harvard University Press, 2010), 245.

"Husband and wife are one person" in William Blackstone, *Commentaries on the Laws of Virginia*, Vol. 1 (1765), 442–445.

Reverend Hugh Peters quoted in Mary Beth Norton, *Founding Mothers and Fathers: Gendered Power and the Forming of American Society* (New York: Knopf, 1996), 359.

Cotton Mather, "A Brand Pluck'd out of the Burning," in *Narratives of the Witchcraft Cases 1648-1706*, ed. George Lincoln Burr (New York: Barnes and Noble, 1946), 267–272.

"'Tis woman's sphere" quoted in Mary Beth Norton, *Separated by Their Sex: Women in Public and Private in the Colonial Atlantic World* (Ithaca, N.Y.: Cornell University Press, 2011), 16.

Chapter 2

Mercy Otis Warren, *Mercy Otis Warren: Selected Letters,* ed. Jeffrey H. Richards and Sharon M. Harris (Athens: University of Georgia Press, 2009), 34.

Abigail Adams quoted in *The Letters of John and Abigail Adams,* ed. Frank Shuffelton (New York: Penguin, 2004), 148.

Mary A. Jones and Lucy Henderson quoted in Lillian Schlissel, *Women's Diaries of the Westward Journey* (New York: Schocken Books, 1982), 28, 50–51.

Gertrude Ella Thomas quoted in *Divided Houses: Gender and the Civil War,* ed. Catherine Clinton and Nina Silber (New York: Oxford University Press, 1992), 7.

Mary Boykin Chesnut, *Mary Chesnut's Civil War,* ed. C. Vann Woodward (New Haven, Conn.: Yale University Press, 1983), 40–41.

Sarah Grimké, Abigail Lyman, and Dorchester Maternal Association quoted in Nancy F. Cott, *The Bonds of Womanhood: "Woman's Sphere" in New England, 1780-1835* (New Haven, Conn.: Yale University Press, 1977), 1, 43, 149.

Sarah Hodgdon quoted in *Farm to Factory: Women's Letters, 1830-1860,* ed. Thomas Dublin (New York: Columbia University Press, 1981), 42.

Frances Trollope quoted in Karin Gedge, *Without Benefit of Clergy: Woman and the Pastoral Relationship in Nineteenth-Century American Culture* (New York: Oxford University Press, 2003), 18.

Susan B. Anthony quoted in Nancy Woloch, *Women and the American Experience: A Concise History* (New York: McGraw-Hill, 1996), 108.

"Moral suasion is moral balderdash" quoted in Lori Ginzberg, *Women and the Work of Benevolence: Morality, Politics and Class in the Nineteenth-Century United States* (New Haven, Conn.: Yale University Press, 1990), 17.

Abby Kelley Foster quoted in James A. Morone, *Hellfire Nation: The Politics of Sin in American History* (New Haven, Conn.: Yale University Press, 2004), 166.

Sojourner Truth quoted in Nell Painter, *Sojourner Truth: A Life, a Symbol* (New York: Norton, 1996), 125–126.

Seneca Falls Declaration of Sentiments, reprinted in *The Concise History of Woman Suffrage*, ed. Mari Jo Buhle and Paul Buhle (Urbana: University of Illinois Press, 1978), 94–98.

"[Largest and highest] Proper Sphere" quoted in Ellen Carol DuBois, *Woman Suffrage and Women's Rights* (New York: New York University Press, 1998), 60.

Margaret Fuller, *Woman in the Nineteenth Century* (New York: Norton, 1971), 37.

Chapter 3

Ida B. Wells, *Crusade for Justice: The Autobiography of Ida B. Wells*, ed. Alfreda M. Duster (Chicago: University of Chicago Press, 1970), 64.

Lucy Buck quoted in Drew Gilpin Faust, *Mothers of Invention: Women of the Slaveholding South in the American Civil War* (Chapel Hill: University of North Carolina Press, 1996), 249.

Louisa May Alcott, *The Journals of Louisa May Alcott*, ed. Joel Myerson and Daniel Shealy (Athens: University of Georgia Press, 1997), 110.

"You may give your Negroes away" quoted in *Early American Women: A Documentary History, 1600–1900*, ed. Nancy Woloch (New York: McGraw-Hill, 2013), 268.

Mary S. Battey quoted in *The Female Experience: An American Experience*, ed. Gerda Lerner (Indianapolis: Bobbs-Merrill, 1977), 238.

Anna Julia Cooper quoted in Paula Giddings, *When and Where I Enter: The Impact of Black Women on Race and Sex in America* (New York: Morrow, 1984), 13.

Agnes Nestor, "A Day's Work Making Gloves," in Nestor, *Woman's Labor Leader* (Rockford, Ill.: Bellevue Books, 1954), 37–41.

"Quit with a headache" quoted in Ellen Carol DuBois and Lynn Dumenil, *Through Women's Eyes: An American History with Documents*, ed. Nancy F. Cott (Boston: Bedford/St. Martin's, 2005), 349.

Mary Elizabeth Lease quoted in *Root of Bitterness: Documents of the Social History of American Women* (Boston: Northeastern University Press, 1996), 414.

Zitkala-Sä (Gertrude Simmons Bonnin), "An Indian Teacher among Indians," *Atlantic Monthly* 85 (March 1900), 385–386.

Sarah Platt Decker quoted in *Writing the Range: Race, Class, and Culture in the Women's West*, ed. Elizabeth Jameson and Susan Armitage (Norman: University of Oklahoma Press, 1997), 372.

Lillian Wald quoted in Robyn Muncy, *Creating a Female Dominion in American Reform, 1890–1935* (New York: Oxford University Press, 1991), 39.

"I have been & gone & done," Susan B. Anthony to Elizabeth Cady Stanton, November 5, 1872, Ida Harper Collection, Huntington Library, San Marino, California.

"All feminists are suffragists" quoted in Nancy F. Cott, *The Grounding of Modern Feminism* (New Haven, Conn.: Yale University Press, 1987), 15.

Rose Winslow quoted in Doris Stevens, *Jailed for Freedom* (New York: Schocken Books, 1976), 191.

Anna Howard Shaw quoted in Alana Jeydel, *Political Women: The Women's Movement, Political Institutions, the Battle for Women's Suffrage and the ERA* (New York: Routledge, 2004), 84.

"Letters of Negro Migrants of 1916–1918," *Journal of Negro History* 4, no. 3 (July 1919), 317.

Chapter 4

Eleanor Roosevelt, *It's Up to the Women* (New York: Frederick A. Stokes, 1933), ix.

Willa Cather quoted in Laura Winters, *Willa Cather: Landscape and Exile* (Selinsgrove: Susquehanna University Press, 1993), 36.

Hattie McDaniel quoted in Emily Yellin, *Our Mothers' War: American Women at Home and at the Front during World War II* (New York: Simon and Schuster, 2010), 222.

Zora Neale Hurston, "How It Feels to Be Colored Me," *World Tomorrow*, May 11, 1928.

Robert S. Lynd and Helen Merrill Lynd, *Middletown in Transition: A Study in Cultural Conflicts* (New York: Harcourt, Brace, 1937), 178–179.

"We had no choice" quoted in Jeane Westin, *Making Do: How Women Survived the '30s* (Chicago: Follett, 1976), 128.

"Few . . . who oppose married women's employment" quoted in Ruth Shallcross, *Should Married Women Work?* (Washington, D.C.: National Association of Business and Professional Women, 1940), 17.

Langston Hughes, *The Big Sea, An Autobiography* (New York: Knopf, 1940), 24.

Monica Sone, *Nisei Daughter* (Seattle: University of Washington Press, 1979), 177–178.

Betty Friedan, *The Feminine Mystique* (New York: Norton, 2001), 91.

Ella Baker quoted in *Women in the Civil Rights Movement: Trailblazers and Torchbearers*, ed. Vicki L. Crawford, Jacqueline Anne Rouse, and Barbara Woods (Indianapolis: Indiana University Press, 1990), 25.

Shulamith Firestone quoted in Nancy Woloch, *Women and the American Experience: A Concise History* (New York: McGraw-Hill, 1996), 367.

"What oppression is comprised of on a day-to-day basis": Barbara Smith, editor's introduction to *Home Girls: A Black Feminist Anthology* (1983; reprint, New Brunswick, N.J.: Rutgers University Press, 2000), xxxiv.

Jessie De La Cruz quoted in Ellen Cantarow with Susan Gushee O'Malley and Sharon Hartman Strom, *Moving the Mountain: Women Working for Social Change* (Old Westbury, N.Y.: Feminist Press, 1980), 134–135, 136, 151.

Phyllis Schlafly, "Sexist Mischief in Schools and Colleges," *Phyllis Schlafly Report* 9, no. 2 (September 1975), sec. 2.

Further reading

Allen, Paula Gunn. *Pocahontas: Medicine Woman, Spy, Entrepreneur, Diplomat.* San Francisco: HarperSanFrancisco, 2003.

Anderson, Bonnie. *Joyous Greetings: The First International Women's Movement, 1830–1860.* New York: Oxford University Press, 2000.

Armitage, Susan, and Elizabeth Jameson, eds. *The Woman's West.* Norman: University of Oklahoma Press, 1987.

Armitage, Susan, and Elizabeth Jameson, eds. *Writing the Range: Race, Class, and Culture in the Women's West.* Norman: University of Oklahoma Press, 1997.

Barr, Juliana. *Peace Came in the Form of a Woman: Indians and Spaniards in the Texas Borderlands.* Chapel Hill: University of North Carolina Press, 2007.

Boydston, Jeanne. *Home and Work: Housework, Wages, and the Ideology of Labor in the Early Republic.* New York: Oxford University Press, 1990.

Brown, Kathleen M. *Good Wives, Nasty Wenches, and Anxious Patriarchs: Gender, Race, and Power in Colonial Virginia.* Chapel Hill: University of North Carolina Press, 1996.

Cobble, Dorothy Sue. *The Other Women's Movement: Workplace Justice and Social Rights in Modern America.* Princeton, N.J.: Princeton University Press, 2004.

Cook, Blanche Wiesen. *Eleanor Roosevelt.* Vol. 1. New York: Viking, 1992.

Cook, Blanche Wiesen. *Eleanor Roosevelt.* Vol. 2. New York: Viking, 1999.

Cott, Nancy F. *The Bonds of Womanhood: "Woman's Sphere" in New England, 1780–1835.* 2nd ed. New Haven, Conn.: Yale University Press, 1997.

Cott, Nancy F. *The Grounding of Modern Feminism.* New Haven, Conn.: Yale University Press, 1987.

Dublin, Thomas. *Women at Work: The Transformation of Work and Community in Lowell, Massachusetts, 1826–1860.* 2nd ed. New York: Columbia University Press, 1993.

DuBois, Ellen Carol. *Feminism and Suffrage: The Emergence of an Independent Women's Movement in America, 1848–1869.* Ithaca, N.Y.: Cornell University Press, 1978.

Edwards, Rebecca. *Angels in the Machinery: Gender in American Party Politics from the Civil War to the Progressive Era.* New York: Oxford University Press, 1997.

Faderman, Lillian. *Odd Girls and Twilight Lovers: A History of Lesbian Life in Twentieth-Century America.* New York: Columbia University Press, 1991.

Faludi, Susan. *Backlash: The Undeclared War against American Women.* New York: Crown, 1991.

Faust, Drew Gilpin. *Mothers of Invention: Women of the Slaveholding South in the American Civil War.* Chapel Hill: University of North Carolina Press, 1996.

Flexner, Eleanor, and Ellen Fitzpatrick. *Century of Struggle: The Woman's Rights Movement in the United States.* Rev. ed. Cambridge, Mass.: Harvard University Press, 1996.

Freedman, Estelle, and John D'Emilio. *Intimate Matters: A History of Sexuality in America.* 3rd ed. Chicago: University of Chicago Press, 2012.

Gabaccia, Donna. *From The Other Side: Women, Gender, and Immigrant Life in the U.S., 1820–1990.* Bloomington: Indiana University Press, 1994.

Gidding, Paula. *When and Where I Enter: The Impact of Black Women on Race and Sex in America.* 2nd ed. New York: Morrow, 1996.

Gilmore, Glenda E. *Gender and Jim Crow: Women and the Politics of White Supremacy in North Carolina, 1896–1920.* Chapel Hill: University of North Carolina Press, 1996.

Ginzberg, Lori. *Women and the Work of Benevolence: Morality, Politics, and Class in the Nineteenth-Century United States.* New Haven, Conn.: Yale University Press, 1990.

Glenn, Evelyn Nakano. *Issei, Nisei, War Bride: Three Generations of Japanese American Women in Domestic Service.* Philadelphia: Temple University Press, 1986.

Gordon-Reed, Annette. *The Hemingses of Monticello: An American Family.* New York: Norton, 2008.

Gutierrez, Ramon. *When Jesus Came, the Corn Mothers Went Away: Marriage, Sexuality, and Power in New Mexico, 1500–1846*. Stanford, Calif.: Stanford University Press, 1991.

Hewitt, Nancy. *Women's Activism and Social Change, Rochester, New York, 1822–1872*. Ithaca, N.Y.: Cornell University Press, 1984.

Horowitz, Daniel. *Betty Friedan and the Making of* "The Feminine Mystique": The *American Left, the Cold War, and Modern Feminism*. Amherst: University of Massachusetts Press, 1998.

Hunter, Tera. *To 'joy My Freedom: South Black Women's Lives and Labors after the Civil War*. Cambridge, Mass.: Harvard University Press, 1997.

Hurtado, Albert L. *Intimate Frontiers: Sex, Gender, and Culture in Old California*. Albuquerque: University of New Mexico Press, 1999.

Hyde, Anne F. *Empires, Nations, and Families: A New History of the North American West, 1800–1860*. Lincoln: University of Nebraska Press, 2011.

Karlsen, Carol. *The Devil in the Shape of a Woman: Witchcraft in Colonial New England*. New York: Norton, 1987.

Kerber, Linda. *Women of the Republic: Intellect and Ideology in Revolutionary America*. Chapel Hill: University of North Carolina Press, 1980.

Kessler-Harris, Alice. *In Pursuit of Equity: Women, Men, and the Quest for Economic Citizenship in Twentieth-Century America*. New York: Oxford University Press, 2001.

Kessler-Harris, Alice. *Out to Work: A History of Wage-Earning Women in the United States*. New York: Oxford University Press, 1982.

Kugel, Rebecca, and Lucy Eldersveld Murphy, eds. *Native Women's History in Eastern North America before 1900: A Guide to Research and Writing*. Lincoln: University of Nebraska Press, 2007.

May, Elaine Tyler. *Homeward Bound: American Families in the Cold War Era*. New York: Basic Books, 1988.

Mead, Rebecca J. *How the Vote Was Won: Woman Suffrage in the Western United States, 1868–1914*. New York: New York University Press, 2004.

Meyerowitz, Joanne, ed. *Not June Cleaver: Women and Gender in Postwar America, 1945–1960*. Philadelphia: Temple University Press, 1994.

Muncy, Robyn. *Creating a Female Dominion in American Reform, 1890–1935*. New York: Oxford University Press, 1991.

Norton, Mary Beth. *Liberty's Daughters: The Revolutionary Experience of American Women, 1750–1800*. Boston: Little, Brown, 1980.

Pascoe, Peggy. *What Comes Naturally: Miscegenation Law and the Making of Race in America*. New York: Oxford University Press, 2009.

Perdue, Theda. *Cherokee Women: Gender and Culture Change, 1700–1835*. Lincoln: University of Nebraska Press, 1998.

Perdue, Theda, ed. *Sifters: Native American Women's Lives*. New York: Oxford University Press, 2001.

Ransby, Barbara. *Ella Baker and the Black Freedom Movement: A Radical Democratic Vision*. Chapel Hill: University of North Carolina Press, 2003.

Rosen, Ruth. *The World Split Open: How the Modern Women's Movement Changed America*. New York: Viking, 2000.

Roth, Benita. *Separate Roads to Feminism: Black, Chicana, and White Feminist Movements in America's Second Wave*. New York: Cambridge University Press, 2004.

Ruiz, Vicki. *From Out of the Shadows: Mexican Women in Twentieth-Century America*. New York: Oxford University Press, 1998.

Schechter, Patricia. *Ida B. Wells-Barnett and American Reform, 1880–1930*. Chapel Hill: University of North Carolina Press, 2001.

Shoemaker, Nancy, ed. *Negotiators of Change: Historical Perspectives on Native American Women*. New York: Routledge, 1995.

Slater, Susan, and Fay A. Yarbrough, eds. *Gender and Sexuality in Indigenous North America, 1400–1850*. Columbia: University of South Carolina Press, 2011.

Solomon, Barbara Miller. *In the Company of Educated Women: A History of Women and Higher Education in America*. New Haven, Conn.: Yale University Press, 1985.

Stansell, Christine. *City of Women: Sex and Class in New York, 1789–1860*. New York: Knopf, 1986.

Stevenson, Brenda E. *Life in Black and White: Family and Community in the Slave South*. New York: Oxford University Press, 1996.

Ulrich, Laurel Thatcher. *Good Wives: Image and Reality in the Lives of Women in Northern New England*. New York: Knopf, 1982.

Ware, Susan, ed. *Modern American Women: A Documentary History*. 2nd ed. Boston: McGraw-Hill, 2002.

White, Deborah Gray. *Ar'n't I a Woman: Female Slaves in the Plantation South*. Rev. ed. New York: Norton, 1999.

Yung, Judy. *Unbound Feet: A Social History of Chinese Women in San Francisco*. Berkeley: University of California Press, 1995.

Index

Note: page numbers in italics refer to illustrations